May

To Jacob
with love,
    Memama and Pop Pop
DC Zoo Visit with Uncle Brady,
Mommy and Peter

Animal Habitats

Sandy Creek
NEW YORK

Sandy Creek
NEW YORK

An Imprint of Sterling Publishing
387 Park Avenue South
New York, NY 10016

Editors Caroline Bingham, Fleur Star,
Zahavit Shalev, Elizabeth Haldane,
Lorrie Mack
Editor, this edition Lorrie Mack

Designers Cathy Chesson,
Jacqueline Gooden, Tory Gordon-Harris,
Karen Hood, Laura Roberts-Jensen,
Mary Sandberg, Clare Shedden
Designer, this edition Hedi Hunter

Consultants Dr. Frances Dipper, Kerstin
Swahn, Julio Bernal, Evan Bowen-Jones,
Ginger Mauney, Berny Sèbe, Bryan and
Cherry Alexander
Consultant, this edition Kim
Dennis-Bryan PhD. FZS

US editor Margaret Parrish
Production editor Siu Chan
Production controller Claire Pearson
Jacket designer Natalie Godwin
Jacket editor Mariza O'Keeffe

Publishing manager Bridget Giles
Art director Rachael Foster
Creative director Jane Bull
Publisher Mary Ling

Previously published as six individual volumes:
*24 HOURS Coral Reef, Rain Forest, Water Hole, Desert,
Mountain,* and *Arctic.*

ISBN: 978-1-4351-5619-7

Manufactured in Hong Kong, China
Lot #:
2 4 6 8 10 9 7 5 3 1
07/14

Contents

Introduction

In every corner of the Earth, millions of enchanting creatures are going about their business every second of every day. In the first light of dawn, for example, fennec foxes are snuggling down to sleep in the desert, while colorful triggerfish are coming out from a crack in the coral reef to search for delicious crabs and snails to eat.

Key to habitats around the world

Tropical forest and rain forest

Temperate forest, including woodland

Coniferous forest, including woodland

Mountains, highlands, rocky slopes

Desert and semidesert

Open habitats including grassland, moorland, heathland, savanna, fields, scrub

Coral reefs and waters immediately around them

Polar regions, including tundra and icebergs

The Arctic

NORTH AMERICA

Tropic of Cancer

Equator

SOUTH AMERICA

Pacific Ocean

Tropic of Capricorn

In each of six chapters (Coral Reef, Rain Forest, Water Hole, Desert, Mountain, and Arctic), you can follow five specific animals as they go through a day and a night, and learn lots of fascinating facts about all the other creatures that share their habitat. Then, as you go through your day—having breakfast, going to school, playing with your friends, eating supper, getting ready for bed—you'll know exactly what all your favorite animals are doing at the same time!

Arctic Ocean   The Arctic

EUROPE

ASIA

Pacific Ocean

AFRICA

Atlantic Ocean

Indian Ocean

AUSTRALIA

ANTARCTICA

Coral Reef

Although they cover less than one percent of the Earth's surface, coral reefs are home to more than 15 percent of all fish species. Welcome to the coral reefs—the fabulous rain forests of the sea.

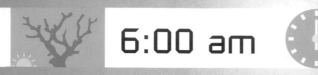

1 Moray eel   2 Butterflyfish   3 Turtle
4 Soft coral   5 Hard coral

Dawn has broken over the "rainforest of the sea," the coral reef. Morning is a busy time on the reef as the fish wake up and begin their search for breakfast.

The **moray eel** is resting in his hole. He constantly opens and shuts his mouth, sucking fresh water over his gills to breathe.

The **turtle** is tired and hungry. She has had a busy night, laying more than 100 eggs on the beach. She's heading for the reef for breakfast.

The **triggerfish** has just woken up and emerged from his crevice. He is ready to go off hunting for crunchy crabs and sea snails.

The **bubble coral** senses it's morning because of the change in light. It has begun to expand its bubbles, or vesicles.

The **reef shark** has had a successful night's hunting. With a full tummy, she's now ready for a rest. She's a big fish, and smaller fish stay clear.

Millions of tiny animals are visible to predators in bright light. During the day, they move down to the **darker depths** of the sea, because they don't want to be eaten. These are the **zooplankton**.

Some zooplankton look like miniatures of the adults they will become, like this shrimp larva.

Don't worry! This planktonic lobster larva is magnified thousands of times.

The bottom of the ladder
Plankton may be small, but without them, the corals and other sea life would not exist. They form the base of the sea's food chain.

"Plankton" comes from a Greek word that means "drifting."

10

Rising to the surface

There are two main types of plankton: phytoplankton and zooplankton. The first are tiny algae cells. Zooplankton are animals – many come up to the sea's surface at night to eat the phytoplankton.

Some plankton have spikes!

Phytoplankton use sunlight to produce much of the oxygen we breathe.

In close-up

Many plankton are so tiny that they can only be seen properly through a microscope. A drop of sea water may hold 100,000 phytoplankton.

The daytime fish are now very active.

They tend to move higher above the coral as the light increases, but are quick to dart back to the safety of holes and crevices in the coral if danger threatens.

There are two main types of corals: hard and soft. **Hard corals** are the reef-building corals and have a protective stony base. Most feed at night. Many **soft corals** feed during the day and sway with the movement of the water. They contribute to the daytime colors of the reef.

A finger-sized squirt can filter a quart (liter) of sea water each hour.

Suck, squirt

Sea squirts show little reaction to changes of light. Day and night, they suck water in through one tube and squirt it out of another.

Soft corals tend to grow on overhangs and cliffs.

Batfish often swim behind turtles, vacuuming up the scraps of food the turtles drop. Black stripes across their eyes help to disguise the vulnerable head: the aim is for the predator to attack the tail, so that the batfish can escape.

There are more than 100 different types of butterflyfish. All have beautiful markings.

Like many reef fish, **butterflyfish** have flattened bodies, perfect for nipping in between the corals. Butterflyfish indicate the health of a reef. The greater the number and variety, the healthier the reef. Butterflyfish often swim in pairs.

It's difficult to see, but a fierce battle is taking place on the reef. **Corals** are always competing for space and light, as are simple reef animals called **sponges**. It can be a battle to the death when one grows over the other.

Corals are animals. Hard corals settle on the sea floor and on slopes.

13

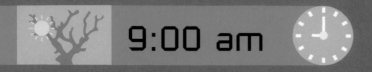
Some fish don't need to hide, even in the bright light of morning. In fact, many fish have odd but effective ways of making sure they don't become a bigger fish's snack. Some have poisonous stingers, while others are just so well camouflaged that they are very difficult to spot.

A large lionfish may come out in the daytime.

Lionfish spines contain poison, and predators learn to avoid them. A lionfish sting can paralyze a fish or even kill it. It can be dangerous for humans, too.

Who's hiding in a crevice? With its long spines, this **porcupine fish** would make a painful meal. It will begin to hunt at night. If threatened, it can expand into a spiky ball.

Frogfish are able to change their color.

The aptly named **boxfish** is an awkward swimmer because it is covered in bony plates that form a tough armor—and not only that, but its skin releases a poisonous mucus.

This spongy-looking creature is a **frogfish**. It's a hard fish to spot, which makes it a good hunter. It can open its mouth—wide!—and suck in a tasty fish in a flash.

An unwary catfish becomes breakfast.

Who's lurking on the bottom? The creepy-looking **crocodile fish** is a clever hunter. It stays dead still. Then, with a snap, a passing fish—or perhaps a crab—is sucked in. It has no warning of its fate.

1 Hard coral **2** Shoaling jacks **3** Turtle

With the sun's rays lighting up the sea, the fish know they are easy targets for a tasty snack. So some group together, seeking the protection of huge schools.

From the safety of his hole, the **moray eel** opens his mouth wide, showing a set of needle-sharp teeth. He can give a nasty bite to an unwary diver.

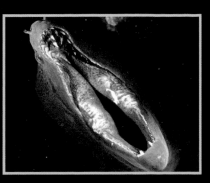

The **turtle** has just popped up to get some air. When awake and moving around, turtles can stay under the water for about 5 minutes.

The **triggerfish** has found his breakfast. He is tackling a prickly sea urchin by flipping the urchin over and attacking the underside.

Now fully expanded, the **bubble coral** shows how it got its name. The delicately patterned bubbles hide the coral's skeleton.

The **reef shark** is still resting. Unlike many sharks, she does this by staying in one place on the bottom.

Bumphead parrotfish spend their days grazing in groups.

Is coral tasty? Parrotfish think so. Having rested all night, they are now hungry and head for the coral. The world's largest parrotfish, the bumpheads, use their heads to loosen bits of coral to eat.

There are about 80 different types of parrotfish. All are very colorful........

CRUNCH

18

Parrotfish take their name from their bright colors, their flapping fins, and their beaks.

From fish to beach

Parrotfish grind down the rocky coral they eat and pass it out as sand. It's amazing, but true, that in this way just one parrotfish creates many pounds (kilograms) of sand each year— sand that finds its way to tropical beaches.

Parrotfish are . . . . . . grazers, and scrape algae off corals. Bumpheads eat the coral, too.

Bony beak

A parrotfish's beak is made of fused teeth. It is an ideal tool for chiseling away at the reef. Parrotfish are sometimes called the "cows of the sea."

Midday and the burning sun is overhead. The promise of a lazy afternoon washes over the reef. The morning rush is over, and there's plenty of time to look at a few of the giants of the reef: the curiously shaped sponges, the giant manta ray, and the amazing giant clam.

The **barrel sponge** may look like a plant, but sponges are simple animals. Sponges are covered in tiny holes through which they draw in water, taking out the food and oxygen they need. Barrel sponges can grow to reach 3 ft (1 m) in height.

Established sponges cannot move, unlike most animals. They feed on tiny particles of food in the water.

Mouth

With a lazy flap of its winglike fins, a **giant manta ray** glides slowly by. From wingtip to wingtip, these creatures can be as wide as a small airplane.

Manta rays are filter-feeders, scooping in plankton-rich sea water. These gentle giants can live for about 20 years.

It's 3 feet (1 m) across and very heavy.

Many people see mollusks every day in the form of slugs and snails. The **giant clam** is also a mollusk. By midday, the clam's shell is wide open, exposing its fleshy lips to the sunlight.

It's early afternoon and time for a wash and brush at the local cleaning station.

A cleaner shrimp's antennae are ideal for probing.

Cleaner wrasse perform a bobbing dance to advertise their services as cleaners.

Cleaning stations do big business on the daytime reef. It's a place where fish and turtles go to get cleaned up.

Table coral provides a good platform for a cleaning station's line.

Cleaning station

Ready for a cleanup

1:10 pm A coral trout is waiting in line for the cleaning station. This large predator will not eat the shrimp that cleans it of parasites.

1:15 pm The trout keeps its mouth wide open while it is being cleaned. It stays motionless to let the cleaner know it will not be harmed.

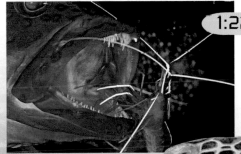

1:22 pm Almost done! Within four or five hours, a couple of hundred fish will have been cleaned.

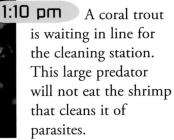

Cleaners are fast workers.

I'll do the mouth!

Two blue-streak cleaner wrasse are busy cleaning away parasites inside the mouth and gills of a big fish called a sweetlips.

1 Turtle   2 Sea fir   3 Manta ray

By 2 pm the reef is a little quieter. The daytime animals have had their breakfast and lunch, and the nighttime animals are still resting. Small fish ignore the passing manta ray, still busy scooping up plankton.

The **moray eel** is taking his turn at the cleaning station. Morays are messy eaters, and they need frequent cleaning.

The **turtle** is nibbling sea grass. Adult green turtles spend lots of their time eating sea grass, mangrove roots, and leaves.

The **triggerfish** is tending to his eggs, and is keeping them clean by blowing sand away. He also blows sand to uncover hidden animals.

A close look at the **bubble coral** reveals tiny creatures living safely among its bubbles—like this little shrimp.

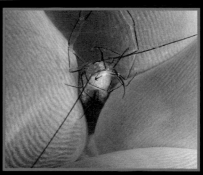

The **reef shark** has found a deep crevice in which to hide. She's still resting—she won't be very active until the sun goes down.

It's **midafternoon** and an anemonefish is hovering above its protective host, a sea anemone. The anemone's tentacles are loaded with stinging cells whose venom is enough to keep most fish away—but not anemonefish, which have a **protective** coat of slime.

Anemone-fish

Some sea anemones close up into a tight ball if threatened.

Anemonefish

Don't come any closer!

This pair of anemonefish is guarding their eggs, laid out of harm's way at the base of their anemone. You can tell which is Mom; the female is always larger than the male.

Anemones are animals and have stinging tentacles...

*Anemonefish swim with **dancing**, **jerky** movements.*

Let's help each other

Anemonefish act as "housekeepers" for their hosts, cleaning up by eating parasites and scraps. In return, the anemone provides a safe haven, and anemonefish rarely stray far from their unusual homes.

Our coral reef, like many other reefs, surrounds a small, low-lying island. The island may be tiny, but it is home to a wide variety of birds, mammals, and reptiles.

A paradise for birds

The island is a good base for birds. Herons and egrets stalk the shores, feeding on fish from the reef. Other birds enjoy the insects and fruits that are found on the island.

Life on the island

 Monitor lizards are meat eaters, and will eat almost anything they find. This one is eating a clutch of turtle eggs.

Coconut crabs are big! They are also called robber crabs because they sometimes steal camping gear, such as batteries or bottles.

The island's fruit bats love sweet, juicy fruit, but also sip nectar from flowers. They tend to feed at night and sleep during the day.

With their bold feathers, Nicobar pigeons are probably the prettiest pigeons in the world. They feed on insects, seeds, and berries.

29

Many sea slugs are smaller than your middle finger.

The sun is now low in the sky, and a colorful collection of sea slugs is grabbing a late afternoon bite. Unlike their drab, land-based cousins, sea slugs brighten up the reef with a kaleidoscope of patterns. Many different varieties can be seen on our reef.

The bright colors shout, "I'm poisonous. Don't touch!"

Most slugs feed during the day and rest at night.

Grub's up

Sea slugs are carnivores, meaning that they eat animals, not plants. They love to munch on sponges or soft corals, and different types are picky about which food they will eat.

Sea slugs breathe through external gills.

Sea slugs are solitary animals, but can sometimes be found in small groups.

What's that?

Believe it or not, sea slugs lay eggs! Most lay them in a long, coiled ribbon, and the eggs are protected from predators and bacteria by a jellylike substance that joins the eggs.

31

Dusk is a dangerous time for the coral fish because their silhouettes are highlighted by the setting sun. There's a lot of activity, with some fish heading for bed and others just waking up.

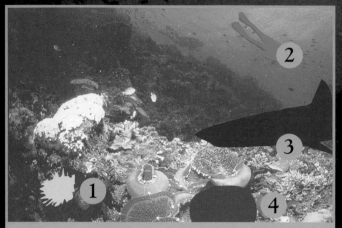

1 Lionfish **2** Scuba diver **3** Reef shark **4** Anemone

The **moray eel** has left his hole and is swimming free. He is now hungry, and dusk is a perfect time for him to hunt.

The **turtle** is looking for a place to sleep. She will soon settle down and, when not moving, can stay underwater for a couple of hours.

The **triggerfish** is relaxing and being cleaned near his nest by a cleaner wrasse. But if a diver disturbs him, he will attack.

The **bubble coral** has reacted to the darkening seas and its bubbles are disappearing, to be replaced by tentacles. It is beginning to feed.

The **reef shark** is cruising along the reef edge. She is looking for an easy meal in the end-of-day rush-hour, but she will ignore the diver.

As **night** falls, the hard corals are transformed into a mass of waving tentacles. Coral reefs are made up of millions of tiny animals called polyps, which look like tiny anemones. The polyp skeletons are all linked together.

A look inside a coral polyp

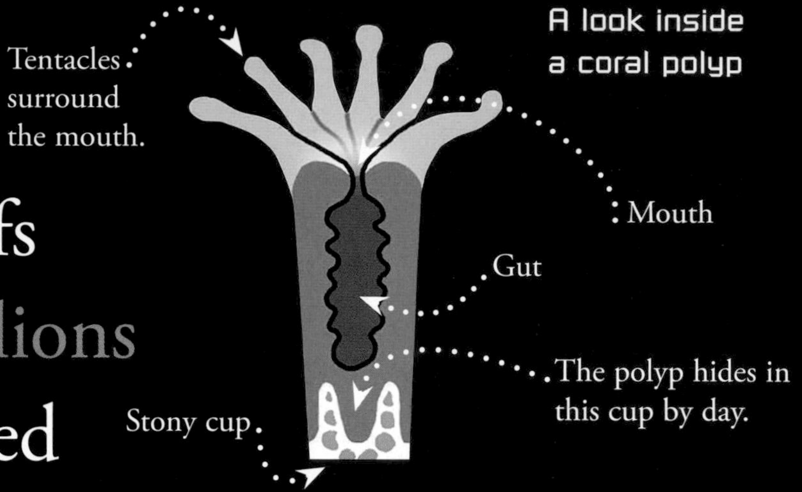

Tentacles surround the mouth.

Mouth

Gut

The polyp hides in this cup by day.

Stony cup.

This staghorn coral has extended its tentacles to feed.

This coral is home to a group of brittle stars. Brittle stars are similar to starfish.

Two butterflyfish nestle in a crevice.

Yellow walls

Tubastrea is a coral that thrives in dark, sheltered places on a reef. It fills the reef walls with a wash of yellow at night, when the tentacles extend to catch passing plankton.

It only takes a minute

Before

Each of the hard coral polyps has spent the day in stony cups. The cups help to protect the soft-bodied polyps.

After

After sunset, the polyps extend their tentacles. Blink and you may miss this. They will spend the night feeding.

Each polyp's tentacles are covered in stinging cells.

It's well into the night and some of the more unusual creatures have begun to appear. A cone shell has crawled out of a coral crevice, while a reef crab pokes around for food. A ghost pipefish drifts silently past two brightly colored mandarin fish.

Harlequin ghost pipefish are strange-looking fish covered in tassels. This disguise makes them difficult to spot when they hide among the frilly arms of feather stars or corals. This pipefish swims with its head down.

They may be beautifully patterned, but **mandarin fish** secrete a disgusting, sticky mucus. A fish that craves a bite of mandarin for dinner won't make the same mistake twice.

Reef crabs come out to hunt at night, but will scurry to a crevice if threatened. This particular type of reef crab is sometimes known as the "seven-eleven" crab because it has seven large spots and four smaller spots (including its eye spots).

This colorful tube is used to sniff out the cone shell's prey.

There are hundreds of different types of **cone shells**, and they are found all over the world. These animals shoot out a "harpoon," or special tooth, from their mouth, which injects a powerful poison. This quickly paralyzes their prey. They are deadly poisonous to humans, too, so never pick one up.

Big eyes for night vision.

Many nighttime fish are

red. In the dark nighttime water, and
in dark caves in the daytime, red fish
appear black, so they are almost
invisible to both prey and predators.
Only flash photography shows their
true color. Many have large mouths
but small teeth, since they feed
mainly on plankton.

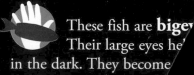

These fish are **bige**
Their large eyes he   m to see
in the dark. They become   the day

38

The winking lights are used to signal other flashlight fish and to confuse predators.

Some fish, such as these **flashlight fish,** can make their own light with the help of bacteria. Flashlight fish live deep down, but rise higher on moonless nights. They can switch off their light by covering it with a skin flap.

Appearance of a Christmas tree

Before This worm has been startled, probably by the photographer, and has withdrawn.

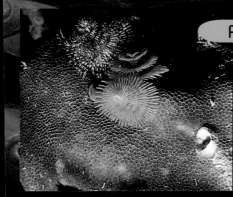

After The worm senses that any danger has gone, and slowly unfolds its pretty tentacles once more.

Christmas tree worms emerge night and day to feed on plankton. As adults, they stay in one place for life.

1 Long-spined sea urchin   2 Glassfish
3 Feather star 4 Double-toothed soldierfish

It is late and the nighttime fish have taken over the reef. Tiny glassfish create a flash of shimmering silver, while a small shoal of soldierfish feast on the plankton that have risen higher in the water.

The **moray eel** has seized his chance and ambushed an unwary fish. Once he has it in his jaws, he will swallow it whole.

The **turtle** has been sleeping on a ledge. She now needs to swim up and take a few gasps of air. Then she will settle down again.

The **triggerfish** is near his crevice. For extra safety, he can wedge himself in by locking his "trigger," a strong spine in his dorsal fin.

During the night, the **bubble coral** sometimes withdraws all its tentacles, as well as its bubbles, revealing its hard skeleton.

The **reef shark** has been joined by others. They will swim over the reef during the night, hunting for fish, and will strike with lightning speed.

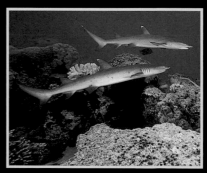

It is now deep into the night and sharks are swimming back and forth over the reef, hunting for food. One of the strangest-looking sharks of all is the hammerhead.

The largest hammerheads grow to more than 13 ft (4-m) in length.

Why a "hammerhead"?
It is thought that the hammerhead's unusual head shape helps this shark sense its prey's position in the water. Sharks do this by picking up small electrical signals that the victim sends out as it moves.

42

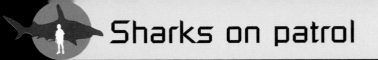

A sea of sharks

Sharks tend to hunt at night in packs, and with hammerheads this can be groups of one hundred or more individuals. They look for fish, lobsters, stingrays, and crabs. If one is successful, there might be a feeding frenzy.

The ray must watch out!

Stingrays have venomous spines near the tips of their tails— but this will not stop a hammerhead shark.

Midnight, and many fish and other creatures are sound sleep or resting. This can be a fairly quiet time on the reef, but some nighttime fish remain active, still feeding under cover of darkness. Restless predators still prowl around, and most small fish stay hidden. Let's take a look around our reef and see what is happening.

Some types of **parrotfish** make a sleeping bag from mucus and spend the night inside. This helps to protect them by stopping predators from picking up their smell.

The **turtle** has to travel to the surface for air every two or three hours, but is otherwise remaining very still. As it sleeps, its eyes will close.

Pinpricks of light occasionally dot the darkened waters. These are because of the tiny, single-celled *Noctiluca*, or **seasparkle**. Under a microscope, *Noctiluca* look like tiny balloons. They sparkle when disturbed.

The big-finned **reef squid** is hunting. This is a well-practiced hunter, and once it has caught a fish, it will chop it up in its strong, beaklike jaws.

Reef squid have eight short tentacles and two long ones for grasping prey.

Garden eels poke a third of their body above their burrows in the sand and pick plankton from the water. They hunt night and day, and retreat quickly if threatened.

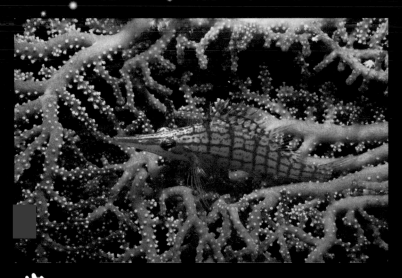

The patchwork-patterned **longnose hawkfish** is a master of disguise. From a distance it can barely be seen against the branching structure of a sea fan.

It's the quiet hours before sunrise, but there's a busy stream of traffic on the reef's island. Hundreds of baby turtles are scrambling toward the sea, having hatched from their eggs. The eggs were laid some 60 days earlier by the turtles' 25-year-old mom.

Sixty days earlier ...

2:00 am The mother turtle dragged herself up the beach and dug a hole for her eggs. It took her a couple of hours to do this.

4:00 am The mother laid about 100 eggs, then covered them up to protect them.

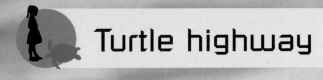
...breakthrough!

I'll come out now!
Baby turtles use a special egg tooth to break out of their soft, leathery egg shell. They can then take a couple of days to dig out of their sandy nest.

The babies head for the sea as fast as they can.

Artificial light can make some babies head the wrong way. They are under immediate threat from ghost crabs, seabirds, and lizards.

47

Rain Forest

As busy as a city, the amazing Amazon rain forest houses

millions of colorful creatures that do lots of the same things we do, like sleep, and eat, and play. Come and explore the biggest jungle in the world!

An emergent tree breaks through the rain-forest canopy.

Dawn is a swift affair in the Amazon, so close to the equator. Sunrise is at the same time all year. As soon as the sun climbs above the canopy, it begins to filter through the trees to warm the forest.

The **jaguar** is settling down to sleep after a successful night's hunting. On lean days, jaguars will continue to hunt through the day.

The **capuchin monkey** is just beginning its day. It moves from its sleeping tree to an eating tree, where it peels the bark, looking for insects.

Scarlet macaws (on left) flock together at the clay lick before breakfast. Eating clay protects them against toxins in the seeds they eat.

The **blue morpho** is pupating—changing from a caterpillar to a butterfly. Its chrysalis has been hanging off of a leaf for a few weeks now.

Hummingbirds are ideal pollinators of **heliconia** flowers. Attracted by the plant's bright red bracts, the birds are rewarded with plenty of nectar.

Howler monkeys are noisy beasts! Having woken the rain forest at dawn with their loud roars, which can be heard 10 miles (16 km) away, they go foraging for breakfast.

Howlers can **hang** upside-down to feast on fruit and **leaves.**

Howler monkeys are territorial—they "howl" to keep other monkeys out.

A baby hangs on to its mother's fur. It is too young to forage for itself.

52

Both red howler and black howler species live in the Amazon rain forest.

Howwlll

Call of nature

The dawn chorus starts with a single male howler's call, which sounds like a breathless bark. Other howlers join in, and the howls grow louder and longer until a roar fills the forest.

Once the macaws

have lined their stomachs with clay, they may fly to a Brazil nut tree for a nutty breakfast. Howler monkeys, sloths, and caterpillars can also be found in the tree's canopy, munching on the juicy green leaves.

No animal could eat Brazil nuts if it weren't for the **agouti**. It is the only creature that can break through the tough outer pod, releasing the nuts inside.

Living for up to 1,000 years, Brazil-nut trees are the oldest in the forest. They are also among the tallest, and can even change the local weather! Together they release enough water from their leaves to form rain clouds.

"I'll **nibble** a few nuts now, and bury the rest for later."

The agouti chisels through the pod with its sharp rodent teeth.

54

Brazil nuts are clustered inside a pod as heavy as a cannonball.

Capuchins drink the nuts' oil as well as eating the kernels.

Bright blue bees are the key to the Brazil nut's success. They are the only insect that can pollinate the tree—and if there is no pollination, there are no seeds and no new trees.

These bees are called orchid bees because they use the scent of orchids to attract mates.

55

A **buzz** of activity surrounds a fig tree, with many different animals turning up to feed on figs. The trees produce fruit all year, even during the dry season when other trees are bare.

The cycle of life

9:15 am Figs can only be pollinated by tiny fig wasps. The female crawls inside through a tiny hole, carrying pollen with her.

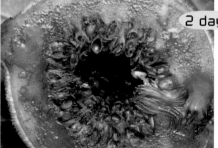

2 days later She lays her eggs inside the fig, pollinating the flowers at the same time. Fig wasps can only reproduce inside figs.

Up to 20 species of fig trees can grow together in the same area of forest, each with its own shape and size of fruit. The largest is the size of a tennis ball.

30 days later The young wasps leave home and fly to another fig to lay their own eggs, taking pollen with them, and the cycle begins again.

A fig is made up of lots of flowers growing inside a skin..

Figs can only ripen if they have been pollinated. The wasps leave the fruit before it ripens.

Vines and lianas grow on most trees in the rain forest, weighing them down and competing for light and nutrients.

Large buttress roots are a sign that the rain-forest soil is shallow. They grow above the ground to keep the tree stable..

More animals eat figs than any other fruit...

Butterflies feast on figs on the forest floor. A butterfly cannot chew; instead, it sucks up fruit pulp through its tube-shaped mouth, called a proboscis.

Safe in its roost, a **tent-building bat** eats a fig fresh from the tree. It carefully peels away the unripe skin with its teeth before eating the seeds inside.

A **coati-mundi** uses its long snout for sniffing out food, but it doesn't need to work hard at foraging when there are easy pickings in the tree.

The strong bill of a **blue and yellow macaw** rips through fig skin easily. Macaws are the only birds that can pick up food in their claws to bring it to their mouths.

1 Jaguar   2 Spider monkey

Midmorning, the sun streams through the trees and heats the forest to 80°F (27°C). An alert jaguar finds a shady spot on the forest floor. It would usually be asleep during the day, but hunger drives it to hunt.

58

Up in a tree, the **jaguar's** spotted fur looks like sunlight shining through the leaves. It has no tree-climbing predators and can sleep safely up there.

Apart from a nap at noon, **capuchins** spend much of the day eating. They are very intelligent and use tools such as stones to crack nutshells.

A **macaw's** strong bill is not just a mouth, it is an extra limb. As well as crushing food, the macaw's bill can grip branches while climbing.

The **blue morpho** chrysalis splits and, after 20 minutes, the imago—adult butterfly—emerges. It then rests for two hours to dry its wings.

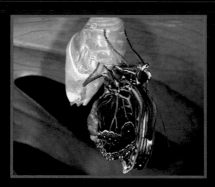

Tent-building bats use large **heliconia** leaves as a daytime roost. They chew the leaves to make them droop, giving shelter from rain, sun, and predators.

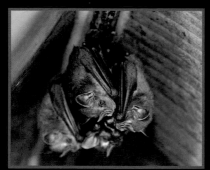

A smash-and-grab raid is taking place in broad daylight. A giant anteater has sniffed out a termite mound, and sits down to dig its snout into a meal. Its long, thin tongue dips in and out of the nest 160 times a minute, scooping up the insects.

Anteaters' long snouts are not just straws for sucking up food; they also use their noses to find ants' nests and termite mounds. They have poor eyesight, so they rely on their sense of smell. If the insects are hard to reach, anteaters will rip the nests apart with their powerful claws.

Azteca ants fight back

11:00 am Azteca ants, a favorite of tamandua anteaters, live inside cecropia tree branches. The tree even provides food for the ants.

1 day later Without damaging the tree, the queen ant lays her eggs inside a narrow stem. It is a home safe from predators.

8 days later In return, the ants attack animals that eat the tree. They can also see off tamanduas with a flurry of bites.

Leafcutter ants stream along the forest floor in a parade of nibbled leaves, carrying them back to their nest.

The ants feed on fungus, which grows on the chewed leaves.

Every rain forest around the world is home to primates, from Asian orangutans to Madagascan lemurs. South America seems to specialize in small monkeys that enjoy playing in the sun!

Tree-dwelling tamarins eat whatever they can find in the canopy, from eggs to fruit.

Spider monkeys have small or no thumbs on their hands: swinging through trees is easier with just four fingers.

Squirrel-sized **tamarins** get around by leaping between trees. They can jump 65 ft (20 m) to the ground and land unhurt.

All **silvery marmosets** are born as twins. They feed on sap straight from the tree.

Spider monkeys are the rain-forest acrobats, active all day and using their tails for climbing. But they do not climb too high in the canopy, to avoid becoming a harpy eagle's lunch.

Only younger woolly monkeys have enough energy to be active at noon. Their parents are resting. Like many larger primates, they prefer a leisurely meal or grooming session to playing.

A **squirrel monkey** pauses in its constant search for fruit to deal with one of the drawbacks of being a furry animal: fleas.

The tail is flexible and acts as a fifth limb.

Bald uakaris have long, red fur everywhere except on their faces. They choose their mates by the color of their face: the redder the head, the healthier and more attractive it is to potential partners.

The smallest monkey in the world, a pygmy marmoset is tiny enough to hide among leaves in the canopy.

A wingspan of 7 ft (2 m) makes this the largest eagle in North and South America.

Each talon is as long as a finger. At 3 in (7 cm) long, the hind talon does the most damage.

It's time for lunch, and a harpy eagle—one of the world's most powerful birds—leaves its chick to hunt for food.

64

The eagle has landed

At last the mother returns to the nest with what's left of the kill, and the chick gets fed. It will not rely on her for long: by the age of ten months, it can hunt for itself.

Watching and waiting

A young chick keeps an eye out for its mother to return from the hunt. Harpy eagles hunt in the canopy, swooping down on a variety of prey, from sloths to snakes.

Small mammals are no problem for a **bill and claws.**

The hooked bill is a vicious tool for ripping into prey.

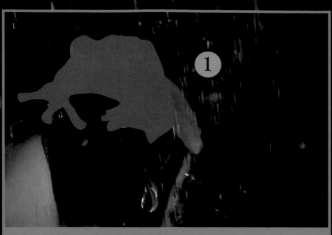

1

1 Red-eyed tree frog

An unexpected heavy rain shower has started. It lasts a brief 30 minutes—but sometimes it rains for days. The rain disrupts life in the canopy, waking a nocturnal frog, which seems happy to take a warm shower.

The **jaguar** has found shelter in dense brush to avoid the rain. A short shower barely reaches the forest floor through the closely growing trees.

The sociable **capuchins** have stopped their daytime grooming and foraging to shelter from the rain. They huddle together for warmth.

Macaws should be out finding food for their chicks, but the rain forces them to stay in their nest. Many chicks starve during heavy rains.

Having dried its wings, which are now bright and shimmering, the **blue morpho** flies down to the forest floor to eat its first meal as an adult.

Rainwater collects in the **heliconia's** bracts, where insects such as mosquitoes lay their eggs. Bigger animals will also drink the water.

The rain has stopped, the heat returns, and the animals reappear. Or do they? Some of them are hard to spot. Insects use camouflage to hide from predators, but iguanas blend in with trees so they can catch insects undetected.

Iguanas also stay hidden to avoid predators. If spotted, they will drop off the branches to escape being caught. Iguanas can fall more than 60 ft (18 m) without being hurt.

The fixed pose of a **praying mantis** can easily be mistaken for a twig.

The underside of a **blue morpho's** wings is not blue, but brown—the perfect camouflage for the forest floor.

Some insects have weird disguises to stay hidden in the daytime.

Spot the difference between the real thorn and the **thorn insect**!

Is this an owl or an **owl butterfly**? The insect has "eye spots" on its wings to confuse and scare off predators such as pacas, which are targets for owls.

Katydids are masters of disguise. A **dead-leaf katydid** becomes part of the forest floor…

…while up in the tree, a **green-leaf katydid** is just one of the crowd.

Lichen grows on some tree trunks. It is a safe home for the spiky **lichen katydid**.

Eek!

A **conehead katydid's** spines are used for defense, but they also help the insect hide among thorns.

Far from hiding in the understory

like insects, birds are a noticeable part of the rain forest. Males are free to show off their bright colors to attract females; at the first sign of a predator, they quickly fly away.

A **toucan** reaches out with its bill to pluck fruit. Its bill is so long, it has to toss its head back and throw the fig into its throat to swallow it.

The **cock of the rock** lives in mountainous parts of the forest. It is vital to the forests because it disperses the seeds of many trees.

The **scarlet tanager** is one of the few rain-forest birds that migrates, spending the summer in North America.

Watch the birdie

The manakin's courtship dance includes raising its tail and cracking it like a whip.

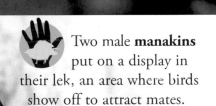

Two male **manakins** put on a display in their lek, an area where birds show off to attract mates.

Of the 27 species of parrots in the rain forest, the **hyacinth macaw** stands head and shoulders above the rest, being 3 ft (1 m) long from head to tail. These macaws are usually seen in the trees, only coming to the ground for food.

Many tank bromeliads grow on trees, using them to get near the sunlight. Other bromeliads live on the ground.

Bromeliads are ideal daytime hideouts for nocturnal frogs. Tiny **red-eyed tree frogs** can rest inside the leaves safe from predators.

In among the trees are thousands of tank bromeliads. They provide a watery home for small animals, and a drinking fountain for larger ones.

Pineapples are bromeliads, but they do not have tanks. The spiky leaves are the beginnings of a new plant.

72

A pygmy marsupial frog carries its tadpoles in its pouch.

Birthing pool

Tadpoles live in water, so most frogs in the Amazon rainforest lay their eggs in bromeliad pools, but some lay on the forest floor. The mother then gives the tadpoles a piggyback ride up to the water.

Bromeliad leaves are stiff and strong, easily taking the weight of a passing **lizard** that has come to drink the water. The nutrients in the water also feed the plant.

Some species of tank bromeliads can hold 12 gallons (45 liters) of water!

The plant's leaves grow in a spiral, with the flowers in the middle. Most only flower once, then die.

73

Rain-forest clouds turn the setting sun's rays into a haze.

The sun sets quickly in the rain forest. There is little time for dusky half-light; as the sun dips behind the canopy, the forest falls dark. It also fills with the sound of frogs, bats, and insects as sunset brings them out for the night.

What's up at 6 o'clock?

The **jaguar** wakes up for the night. After a quick wash, it begins to prowl for food on the ground. It is also an expert tree-climber and swimmer.

Capuchins are getting ready for bed. They search the trees, partly foraging for supper, and partly to find a safe bed for the night.

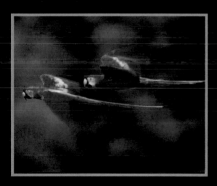

Scarlet macaws are active again now that the rain has dried up. They mate for life and are often seen flying around the forest in pairs.

The **blue morpho** smells the air with its antennae, searching for more food. It will check out new fruit by landing on it and tasting it through its legs.

The **heliconia** has yet another visitor. This time, an ant has been attracted to the sweet nectar and crawls inside the flower for a drink.

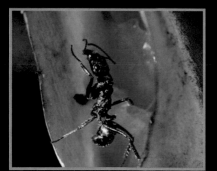

Sunset has brought a shift change for the frogs of Central America and the Amazon rain forest. Diurnal frogs go to sleep at dusk. By 7 pm, the nocturnal tree and leaf frogs are noisily patrolling the canopy, their huge eyes able to see prey—and predators—in the dark.

Poison-dart frogs disappeared at dusk…

Bright colors warn that an animal is poisonous. A **golden** poison-dart frog is extremely toxic.

Poison-dart frogs, like the **blue**, release toxins through their skin when threatened.

A single frog, such as this **green-and-black**, has enough poison to make 50 poison darts.

Strawberry poison-dart frogs are among the smallest frogs of all: just 1 in (2 cm) long.

Heliconias make great lookout posts. Look out, katydid, it's after you! for bug-spotting.

Not all forest frogs live in trees. Among the leaves on the forest floor, a **horned frog** scares off attackers with a display of roaring.

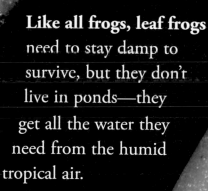

Like all frogs, leaf frogs need to stay damp to survive, but they don't live in ponds—they get all the water they need from the humid tropical air.

There are more than 300 species of frogs in the Amazon.

Leaf frogs do not have webbed feet, but have disks on the ends of their toes to help them grip branches.

77

Listen carefully and among the nighttime noises of the forest are lots of high-pitched clicks: the bats are out. Insect-eating bats appear first; they have been flying around since dusk. Fruit-eaters come out last.

Vampire bat

Vampire bats really do drink blood, but their saliva contains anesthetic so the bite can hardly be felt.

Fringe-lipped bats and other frog-eaters can hear the difference between poisonous and safe frogs by their calls.

Hairy-nosed bats are just one species of insect eater. Imagine tracking a tiny, moving insect only using echoes!

Tent-building bats look for food using both smell and a series of clicking sounds that echo off solid objects like fruit.

Some bats have such large ears

78

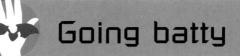
A sac-winged bat is among the first to leave its daytime roost as the sun sets. The insect-hunter lives in groups of up to 50 bats that roost on the buttress roots of trees.

The bones that stretch out the wing are the bat's fingers. The wing itself is made of skin.

How to go fishing without a net

8:29 pm A low-flying fishing bat searches the river for minnows. Its echolocation works through the water.

8:30 pm In the blink of an eye, the bat swoops in on its prey and scoops up the unsuspecting fish in its claws.

they can hear insects without using echolocation.

Carnivorous bats track their prey using echolocation. They send out a click and listen for the echo to return. If it returns quickly, that means something is nearby.

Leaf-nosed bats click through their large, pointed noses. The clicks are louder than those made by bats that use their mouths.

Sloths sleep for 15 hours a day, yet they are barely more active when awake. They move most at night, when they are less visible to predators.

A baby sloth hitches a ride on its mother's stomach until it is strong enough to hang from branches.

Going green
Algae grows in the sloth's long fur, especially in the rainy season. It provides useful camouflage for the slow-moving animal.

Sloths eat only leaves, which don't provide much energy.

Just hanging around
With their long legs and hooked claws, sloths are built for life in the trees. Their front legs are so long that they cannot walk properly on the ground.

Coming down to earth

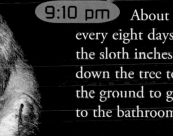

9:10 pm About every eight days, the sloth inches down the tree to the ground to go to the bathroom.

Sloths look like they are grinning all the time. To save energy, they don't ever change their expression.

9:30 pm Once on the ground, the sloth defecates at the base of the tree. The dung is good fertilizer for the tree.

9:35 pm Sloth moths live in the sloth's fur, leaving it only to lay their eggs and feed on the dung.

81

1 Paca   2 Common lancehead snake

A startled paca stops in its tracks as it spots a camouflaged snake while out foraging. The highly poisonous common lancehead detects prey through the heat the animal gives out, and strikes with extreme speed.

The **jaguar** is well into its hunting. It is not a picky eater and does not search out particular prey, but will eat anything it comes across.

Capuchins sleep in small groups in tall trees. They pick a tree that is near a fruit tree, so they do not have to travel far for breakfast in the morning.

Before going to sleep, **scarlet macaws** inspect their nests. Tonight they have spotted signs of a predator and, one by one, the flock flees.

Blue morphos spend their nights hanging from the underside of leaves. They sleep in groups, returning to the same place every night.

Stiff **heliconia** stems are perfect for snakes to wrap around, poised to strike at prey. The big, strong plants are also ideal for frogs to hide in.

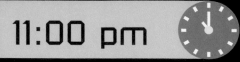
There are two types of spiders: those that spin webs, and those that hunt down prey. Both thrive in the night-time Amazon.

Brazilian huntsman spiders are the most poisonous in the world. They have enough poison to kill 225 mice—in one bite!

 Tarantulas live in burrows, emerging at night to hunt insects. Their massive fangs bite down on prey, injecting poison into the victim.

Dinner is always a social occasion.

Most spiders live alone, even killing and eating each other. Not so **social spiders**. They build massive, shared webs. Working together, they can catch prey that is more than 10 times bigger than they are.

A single web can contain hundreds of social spiders.

Dinner's ready, hop to it!

Before A **jumping spider** can leap 50 times the length of its body. This one spots its prey on a nearby leaf and makes a short hop…

After …to land right on top of the unsuspecting bug. It quickly kills its prey and digs in to dinner.

Some orb weavers await prey sitting in the middle of their webs; others sit at the edge.

An orb weaver spins its round, sticky web in an open space between trees. It's a perfect place for careless insects to fly into the trap.

Under cover of darkness, small mammals go about their business of finding food while trying to avoid predators. It is not easy to see in the dark forest, so many rely on their sensitive whiskers to feel their way.

Kinkajous live entirely in the trees, surviving mostly on fruit. Sometimes called "night walkers" because they are seen at night, they are also heard chattering, calling, and making "kissing" sounds when happy.

Kinkajous have good night vision. The lining in the back of their eyes reflects light, making them glow in the dark.

Kinkajous bite straight to the nectar, which they lap up with their incredible 5-in- (13-cm-) long tongues. That's like a human child having a tongue 9 in (23 cm) long!

An emerald tree boa scoops up an opossum in a swift, silent strike, swallowing it head-first.

Despite being rodents and related to mice, **pacas** are bigger than cats—yet they eat just seeds and fruit, picked up during nighttime foraging. They spend their days inside a burrow, safe from predators behind a wall of leaves at the entrance.

Opossums are marsupials—the females carry their young in a pouch. The tiny babies crawl there at birth and stay, feeding, for three months. Then they move to her back.

A carnivorous **mouse opossum** emerges from her underground burrow to go hunting with the family. In 10 days, the babies will grow too heavy to carry and be able to hunt for themselves.

It's been a long night

of hunting for the jaguar. Finally, it catches an armadillo, killing it with one bite to the head.

The jaguar's name comes from the Mayan word *yaguar*, which means "he who kills in one leap."

Jaguar cubs live with their mother until they are two years old. In that time, she teaches them hunting skills. Even brotherly, playful wrestling is useful practice in fighting prey.

Cat cousins

Jaguars are not the only nocturnal cats. Their smaller relatives, ocelots and margays, are busy hunting prey such as frogs, insects, and monkeys.

Killer instinct

The Americas' largest cat has a fearsome bite—the second-strongest of any mammal. An armadillo's plates are no problem for its jaws.

Margays are small, arboreal cats that move around the trees much like monkeys, leaping between branches and gripping them with their paws.

Ocelots have excellent night vision, hearing, and sense of smell, which they use for tracking prey from the ground, trees, or rivers.

Water Hole

A life-giving oasis in a parched landscape, the water hole is an incredible place—during the course of a day, hundreds of creatures visit it to drink, eat, bathe, and just hang out.

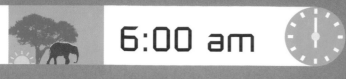

1 Elephant

T he chilly night is over, but the sun hasn't come up yet. A troop of elephants gathers around the water hole. Sometimes, elephants dig for water in dry riverbeds—if they find it, other animals will benefit too.

The **lion** and **lioness** lap at the water's edge following a night spent hunting and feasting. After a drink, they will doze the morning away.

Zebras and other herd animals make way when predators want to drink. They keep a lookout for one another just in case anyone else is still hungry.

The **giraffes** take their time at the water hole, chewing leaves— something they do for at least 12 hours a day— while they wait to drink.

The **African harrier hawk** returns to her nest hidden in a craggy rock face far from the water hole. Her chicks cheep urgently for food.

The **elephant** digs in the soil for salt, an important part of its diet. Young elephants learn where the salt is buried from older members of the herd.

Elephants live in herds made of females and their children. The oldest and most **knowledgeable** elephant is in charge. She could be as old as 60. Males **leave** the herd at about 13 years old and sometimes form their own **bachelor** herd.

Pregnancy in elephants lasts almost two years, so babies don't come along that often.

The trunk is as useful to an elephant as your hands are to you...

Despite their **size** elephants are gentle...

94

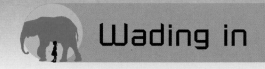
Elephant skincare

If these elephants look a little dusty, that's because they are! After bathing, elephants suck dust into their trunks and then dump it all over their bodies. It acts as an insect repellent, and stops the sun from damaging their skin.

Bathtime for a baby elephant

10:02 am This baby elephant is feeling a bit uncertain about getting into the water and dithers hesitantly at the water's edge...

10:03 am A caring, motherly trunk reaches out. It first coaxes, and then gently pushes, the little elephant in.

10:25 am Once in the water, all fears are forgotten. Adults and baby play contentedly in the cool water.

...but these springboks scramble out of the way when they approach!

Elephants are very steady because they always have three feet on the the ground...

The area surrounding the water hole is patterned with paths the elephants have created as they travel between the water hole and the forested areas where they go to eat leaves.

Insects and other creatures disturbed by the elephants' heavy tread are swiftly snapped up by waiting birds..

Elephants walk at a leisurely 3 miles (5 km) per hour, but they per hour if they need to!

Elephants can communicate with each other over distances as far as 1½ miles (2.5 km). We can't hear these sounds, so it surprises us when many elephants suddenly arrive at the water hole at the same time.

Recycling elephant dung

8:10 am Since it doesn't digest its food fully, a lot of useful matter remains in the 220 pounds (100 kg) of dung produced by an **elephant** each day.

8:20 am First to arrive are **butterflies**. They cluster around the fresh dung and suck out the nutritious liquid.

10:00 am Birds eat the seeds contained in the dung, and pluck out undigested grass and straw to use in building their nests.

5:00 pm Dung **beetles** form the dung into small, compact balls. They determinedly roll these to their tunnels and lay eggs on them.

11:00 pm If what remains by now is damp enough, **mushrooms** may start to sprout from the dung pile. That means food for yet more animals.

can **run** at 25 miles (40 km)

97

There's safety in numbers for the members of a herd. If you're a strong healthy animal and a hungry lion appears while you're grazing, there's a good chance the unlucky victim will be someone else!

Most grazing animals drink at least once every day, so they can't stray far from the water hole. The tracks they make as they travel between feeding grounds and the water hole are etched into the landscape.

When food is scarce, impalas have less energy, and so are more vulnerable to predators.

If attacked, this tranquil herd of impalas will EXPLODE into a chaotic frenzy of leaping to CONFUSE their attackers.

Peculiar-looking wildebeest wander over vast distances in search of grass and water.

Home on the plains

8:00 am Zebras live in family groups. They graze together and groom one another by nibbling at each other's backs and manes.

8:35 am Two males rear up, kicking and biting each other. They are competing to head the group and breed with the females.

8:41 am Relatively few foals are killed by predators—they are all born at the same time so there are lots. Also, the herd protects them well.

8:56 am Sensing danger, they scatter. Stripes make it harder for a predator to single out an individual.

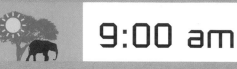

1 Combretum tree **2** Giraffe
3 Guinea fowl **4** Zebra **5** Springbok

Midmorning at the water hole and it's busy, but the animals line up patiently to wait their turn. Fights hardly ever break out because everyone knows the rules and makes way for the elephants.

100

What's up at 9 o'clock?

The **lions** are still relaxing. They don't have to be constantly alert because, at the top of the food chain, there is no one to prey on them.

The **zebras** are milling around near the water. Their striped coats dazzle their enemies and may also help them cope with the extreme heat.

Play-fighting between young male **giraffes** is called sparring. They interlock necks and struggle together—sometimes they get hurt.

In the branches of a tree, the **harrier hawk** looks for food. As well as small animals, she will eat palm nut husks if she can find them.

Dust baths are a fun and important part of the **elephant's** routine. The dust gives the elephant its familiar dusty look.

There's plenty of high drama low down. Smaller predators like hyenas and jackals win their prey more with daring than with muscle, while rodents and insects spend time both above and below ground.

Bat-eared foxes listen for insects beneath the soil and then snap them up.

Dung beetles collect animal droppings and take them home as food.

Termites live in enormous underground colonies and eat dead and rotting matter.

The pack can take on and bring down a large animal like a

Cape ground squirrels live underground where it's quite chilly. They dig for roots and bulbs, and come up to the surface to sunbathe.

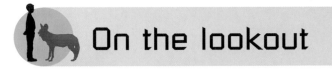

On the lookout

Spotted hyenas sometimes hunt alone but usually do better by cooperating and hunting in packs.

zebra or even a wildebeest.

Providing food for the family

10:29 am Black-backed jackals will eat most things. A jackal attacks a flock of sand grouse by the water's edge, making them scatter.

10:33 am Having caught and killed a bird, this jackal has to avoid having its prize snatched away by bigger predators on the way home.

10:40 am Three hungry cubs are waiting for their share back at the den. In a few months, they, too, will be out hunting for food.

It's great being tall. Giraffes can reach the juicy leaves at the top of the tree and see hungry lions a long way off. But there's at least one big disadvantage—it's a long way down to get a drink.

Responsible drinking

11:02 am It's safe to drink, so this giraffe starts to move its front legs apart.

Giraffes roam in small herds of between three and 20 animals with no obvious leader.

Tall tales

This giraffe is taller than three tall men standing on each other's heads!

A giraffe has just **seven** bones in its neck, the **same** number as you.

Looking out for danger

Bending over is tricky, and getting up is even harder. A thirsty giraffe can spend hours making sure it's absolutely safe before quenching its thirst.

11:08 am Long legs move out some more and then the head goes down.

11:15 am One-way valves in the giraffe's neck stop blood from suddenly flooding its brain.

Midday

The birds that visit the water hole are extremely varied. They range from enormous ostriches to tiny oxpeckers, flesh-eating storks to insect-crunching hornbills, and group-loving guineafowl to solitary storks.

Delicate and pretty they may be, but **lilac-breasted rollers** make a surprisingly harsh squawking sound!

Oxpeckers and giraffes form an **unlikely** partnership. The little birds keep the giraffes free of **ticks** and **fleas**.

Oxpeckers have been known to take advantage of their host by keeping the giraffe's insect wounds open so they can feed on its blood.

Ostriches are the largest birds in the world. They don't need much water but they travel far in search of food even though they are unable to fly.

The beak is mostly hollow so it is not as heavy and bulky as it looks.

Perched on top of an anthill, a Marabou stork surveys the area. The thousands of ants living here have nothing to fear – the stork is only interested in eating meat.

In many parts of the world people keep guineafowl so they can eat them.

This bush cricket's defence is the **stink** it gives off when attacked.

This **yellow-billed hornbill** uses its beak to grab and eat seeds and insects—including spiders and scorpions—from the ground.

Guineafowl live in large flocks. By day they peck at the ground in search of food. At dusk their cackle can be heard as they settle for the night.

1 Gemsbok   2 Springbok

It's the hottest time of the day, and the water hole resembles a swimming pool. Animals wade into the water and bathe, just passing the time until the temperature cools down.

Lion cubs scramble playfully over the **lioness**. They are practicing the skills they will use when they come to hunt as adults.

The **zebras** spend calm hours grazing at the dry, yellowish grass. Their diet consists almost entirely of grass with a few leaves and buds.

One of the **giraffes** crunches a bone. This is unusual—they prefer leaves—but bones do provide a good source of calcium.

Soaring high above the water hole, the **harrier hawk** seems to be tossed around by currents of air, but her flight is actually very stable.

The **elephant** plays in the water to keep cool. Its trunk can hold 2½ gallons (10 liters) of water and is a powerful water pistol!

A **combretum** tree provides more than **shade**— its leaves, flowers, seeds, and roots are a baboon **banquet!** Baboons also eat whatever wanders by. Insects, birds, lizards, and small animals should beware if they don't want to become somebody's **lunch.**

The adults sit quietly—it is really too hot to be rushing around.

Babies catch a ride on their mothers' backs.

Young baboons playfully chase one another up the branches of a tree, and scamper around the trunk.

One of the gang

Being a baboon means doing everything together. Baboon gangs sleep in the same tree, and spend their days nearby looking for food, and drinking at the water hole.

During a friendly grooming session, the baboon doing the grooming gets to eat all the juicy bugs it finds!

During grooming, baboons lick each other. They love the salty taste.

The relatively few trees dotting the landscape have very deep roots that enable them to survive long periods with no rain. Their leaves and fruit provide food for a variety of insects, birds, and small animals.

Sociable weaver birds build enormous nests. Each bird has its own "apartment."

Black mambas can MOVE as fast as you can run. And their venom is deadly.

About 40 baboons sleep at this baboon base camp and spend the day on the ground nearby.

Clever killers

Boomslangs climb trees and slither between branches to catch lizards and even birds. They strike at their prey, injecting it with poisonous venom.

Skinks scuttle around looking for spiders and insects to eat. If attacked, a skink can shed its tail in order to make a quick getaway.

This mother **scorpion** carries her babies on her back. Over time, their exoskeletons (bony coverings) will gradually darken and harden.

Unusually for an owl, the **pearl-spotted owlet** often hunts by day. Despite its small size, it is very strong and isn't afraid to attack prey bigger than itself.

Combretum trees can grow very large. Rhinos love to munch on the young leaves. As the tree grows older, deep cracks form in the bark, which will provide homes for many small creatures.

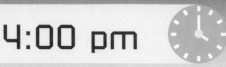

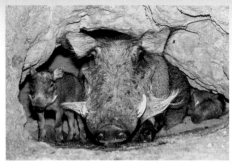

Warthogs normally live in burrows that have been dug by other animals.

The dusty earth looks uninviting, but many insects and reptiles find somewhere to live and a plentiful supply of food on or just below the ground. When the heat gets unbearable, they sit it out underground or in water and wait for cooler days.

Impressive tusks are used for defense against lions and leopards. The lower set is very sharp.

Two pairs of bumpy "warts" between eyes and tusks give this peculiar-looking animal its name.

Like their piggy cooling wallou

Wet and dry survival strategies

Bullfrogs live underground during very dry periods so as not to dry out.

The forked tongue of the **rock monitor lizard** has no taste buds, but it can detect nearby prey by picking up scent particles in the air.

Rhinoceros beetles can carry 100 times their own weight, which makes them the strongest animals on Earth.

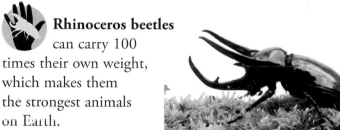

The most remarkable feature of the flap-necked chameleon is its tongue. The same length as the chameleon's body, it is spring-loaded and also equipped with a sucker. Needless to say, it is remarkably effective at snatching and gobbling up insects.

Female **leopard tortoises** bury their eggs in damp ground. During dry weather, they urinate on the earth to make it soft enough.

relatives, warthogs adore a n a muddy pool.

Terrapins are turtles that live in water. They start life eating insects, but later turn to underwater plants and seaweed.

At sunrise, the whole mob emerges from their chilly burrow to warm up!

Sun-loving meerkats live in vast **underground** dens. Each member of the **mob** has a job. Baby-sitters in the den watch over the little ones, sentries outside keep a lookout for **danger**, hunters find food, and teachers **train** young meerkats to hunt.

Cooperation is the name of the game in a meerkat mob. Hunters always bring their food home to share.

Meerkat madness

Look out!

Sentries cheep or cluck if they sense danger, and bark or growl more alarmingly if a hawk or jackal approaches. Everyone instantly dives for cover.

At the **lookout post**, sentries perch on their hind legs, using their **tails** for balance.

Meerkat munchies

 Powerful front claws make digging up **beetles** a snap!

Worms, along with beetles, spiders, and other bugs, are an important part of the meerkat diet.

 Scorpions are gulped down before they can bite. Or perhaps meerkats are immune to venom.

Bolt-holes mean meerkats can make a swift exit if danger looms.

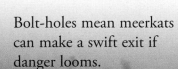

1 Leopard   2 Lion

Dusk descends quickly at the water hole. The large predators such as lions and leopards perk up as the temperature cools down. A pride of lions sharpen their claws on a convenient tree trunk.

118

There is usually one adult male **lion** (alpha male) in a pride, but sometimes there are two—often brothers. Alphas mark their territory with urine.

The **zebras** head for the clearing where they will spend the night. They won't go farther than 7 miles (12 km) from the water hole.

This **giraffe** is still feeding on leaves as the sun sets. Male giraffes are taller than females so they don't compete for the same leaves.

Hovering under a sociable weaver's nest and using a leg to investigate, the **harrier hawk** looks for eggs or chicks to eat.

The **elephant's** trunk reaches out and expertly strips trees of leaves and branches. An incredible 50,000 muscles make it a very precise tool.

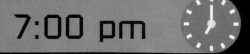
Roaring, not purring

 Cheetahs are built for speed, not strength, so they don't always manage to keep their prey once they have caught it.

Caracals mostly eat birds and mice. They can spring as high as 10 ft (3 m) into the air to swipe and grab at birds as they fly past.

 Lions are the most sociable of the big cats. They live in groups, known as prides, whose members cooperate by hunting together.

From high up in a tree, a **leopard** can suddenly and quietly drop down for the kill.

 **Servals** usually hunt at dusk, leaping up high and whacking their prey with their forepaws.

Most cats, with the exception of lions, live and hunt alone. They stalk their prey by silently creeping around close to the ground and then suddenly pouncing. Some pin their victim down, strangle it, and finish the job with a lethal bite to the windpipe. Others bite the back of the prey's neck, or suffocate it.

Cheetahs are the **fastest** animals on Earth. They can run at **62 miles** (100 km) per hour but only for

Once a leopard has caught its prey, it drags it up a tree. A hungry leopard eats there, away from scavenging jackals and hyenas. If it's not hungry, the meat is hidden away for later.

30 seconds at a time.

The cheetah's long tail helps it make sudden sharp turns while giving chase.

Cats' eyes work very well at night. Cats see as clearly by starlight as a human sees by daylight.

121

After a kill, lions gobble down their food and then spend a day or so on a long after-dinner doze. They can afford to do this because no other animal dares to attack a lion, and anyway, it's a good way to pass the time between meals...

The job of the alpha male is to guard the pride and its territory.

The core of the pride are the 4–6 related lionesses who give birth at around the same time and care for each other's cubs.

Fresh meat for dinner

8:03 pm After many hours in wait, a lioness selects her target—one of the weaker kudus in the herd.

8:04 pm She runs powerfully toward her victim. Panicking, the kudu notices too late and tries to flee.

8:05 pm The lioness grabs the kudu. With a swipe at the legs and a bite to the spine, this kudu stands no chance.

8:15 pm Other lions who joined in the hunt dig in for a big meal. The next few hours will be spent digesting!

Yawnnnnn

When a lion yawns, rather than roars, you can see its enormous tongue. This is so rough that it can scrape meat from bones.

Lion cubs in the lair greet their mother excitedly on her return from a hunting trip. She leads them to her kill for a share of the meat.

123

Lions prefer fresh meat, but the leftovers don't just lie around decomposing. Scavengers polish them off. They'll eat anything that was once alive! As nature's garbage collectors and recyclers, they consume every last scrap of flesh and bone left by the big hunters.

The **lion** in the pride hangs back. He watches distance and then **barges**

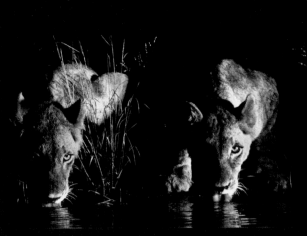

Lionesses drink after a kill. Although they are the hunters and actually do all the hard work, the males of the pride usually eat first, followed by the lionesses, and then the cubs.

the **action** lazily from a

in to get the first bite!

This wildebeest will be just a skeleton within a few hours. Only a very hungry hyena would devour the bones.

Enough for everybody

9:14 pm High in the sky, **African white-backed vultures** use their amazing eyesight to spot the dead wildebeest far below. They make cackling and hissing sounds as they feast.

9:21 pm **Hyenas** arrive as the vultures leave. They bolt their food down, eating as much as a third of their own body weight, before trotting off across the plains.

9:25 pm **Lappet-faced vultures** scare the hyenas away. By ripping through the wildebeest's hide with their hooked beaks, they make it easier for other scavengers to feed next.

9:46 pm **Black-backed jackals** eat quickly, expecting to be pushed out of the way when larger scavengers arrive. Back in their den, they regurgitate some food for their young.

9:50 pm **Marabou storks** pick at the flesh of the wildebeest. They are bald so there are no feathers to get messy when they poke their heads into the rotting carcass.

1 Rhinoceros   2 Giraffe

Late at night the rustling of the undergrowth signals the arrival of rhinos and giraffes. Many other large animals, including elephants and lions, also come to drink during the cool hours of darkness.

The **lions** tear into an unfortunate impala. They eat as much as they can, since it may be another couple of days before their next kill.

The **zebras** huddle together at night. They lie down to sleep, but there are always some members of the herd awake, alert for danger.

The **giraffes** look wide awake. They bend their heads back against their bodies and sleep deeply for just a few minutes each night.

The **harrier hawk** spends some of the night in her nest, but also goes out hunting when her unsuspecting prey is resting.

The **elephant** needs around 50 gallons (200 liters) of water every day. To get its fill, the elephant spends much of the night drinking.

By day, colonies of fruit bats dangle **upside down** in trees.

This spotted eagle owl has excellent hearing. It can hunt in almost total darkness.

Predators,

whether large or small, usually favor nighttime for hunting. It's less tiring to give chase during the cool night, and prey might be asleep, so there's also the advantage of that element of surprise...

Black-backed jackals are determined hunters but will take advantage of any opportunity to scavenge a meal.

At night, they **swarm out** squeaking and whistling in search of fruit to eat.

Owls see well by day and night, but they have to swivel their heads because they can't move their eyeballs.

An unfortunate mouse barely has time to realize what's happening. This barn owl suddenly and silently grabs and kills it, swallowing it whole—fur, bones, and all. In a few hours, the owl will produce a pellet from its mouth containing the parts it is unable to digest.

Nightjars feed on insects, literally grabbing them as they fly by.

Black rhinos have small eyes and poor eyesight but very sensitive hearing and smell. They tend to spend the day resting in the shade and feed at night. When two meet each other at a water hole, they huff and snort, kick up the dust, and then generally ignore each other.

Lions sometimes attack small, adolescent black rhinos, but they don't usually go for adults unless they are old or sick.

There's just not enough vegetation available to support many black rhinos, so each animal lives alone, marking out its territory with urine and dung to keep others away. A pair of rhinos are usually a mating couple who will stay together for a few days, or a mother and her calf.

Giraffes and elephants are often at the water hole in the middle of the night. They sleep far less than humans—about five hours out of 24—and spend almost all of their waking hours eating. Elephants are particularly frequent visitors, since they need to drink as much as 50 gallons (200 liters) a day.

The hooked lip of the black rhino is useful for pulling leafy branches into its mouth.

131

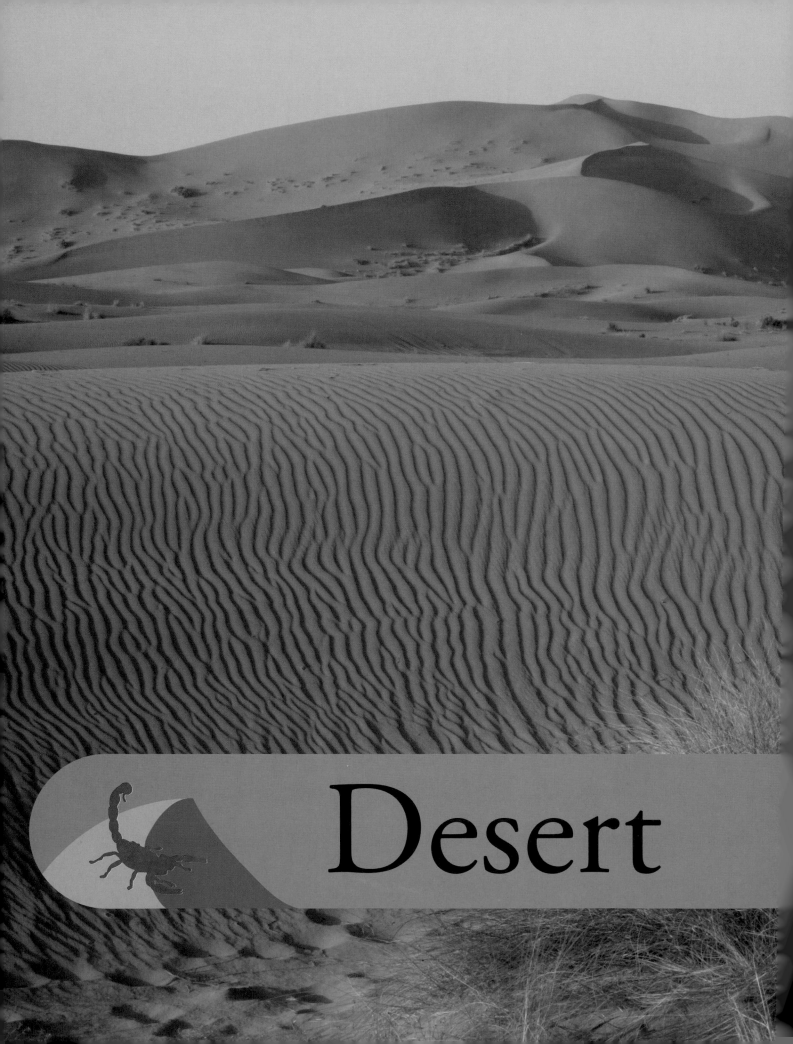

Desert

Among the sand and rocks in this vast, apparently empty space, there's a surprising amount of life. Turn the page and learn about the animals of the Sahara—an arid desert that's as big as Europe.

The desert is quiet in the dawn chill, but in a few minutes it will be much busier.

The cold desert night comes to an end as the Sun rises over the sand dunes, bringing heat to the dry land. The daytime animals begin to stir; they need to get their food for the day before the desert gets too hot.

Fennec fox cubs are settling down to sleep in their den. They have spent the night feeding from their mother while their father was hunting.

As the Sun's rays heat the sand, the nocturnal **horned viper** finishes a night's hunting and warms itself before heading for bed.

A dozing, murky-colored **agama** sunbathes on a rock to raise its temperature. It needs to be warmed up before it becomes active.

In the morning the desert grasses and shrubs are heavy with dew. By grazing now, the **dorcas gazelle** takes in the moisture on the grass.

Already on the move, the **camel** has only had a few hours' rest overnight. It can keep active for 24 hours at a time, but will need to rest afterward.

It's hard to find water in the dry desert. Grazing mammals get moisture from plants when there is no water around for drinking. The best time for eating is first thing in the morning, when the temperature is cool and the grass is wet with dew.

Many desert animals, not just mammals, feed in the morning, before it gets too hot. A **darkling beetle** tips its head down to drink the dew off its own back.

Most of the Sahara's grazing mammals live in herds, and these domestic **sheep** are no exception. They live in the northern desert, where it is easier to find food in the cooler mountains.

Camels have built-in pantries. Their humps contain fat, which they feed off when food is sparse. But they really load up when they find water, drinking up to a quarter of their body weight at one time and storing it in their stomachs.

Both the **male** and **female** addax have long, thin, **spiraling** horns.

The coat of an addax is white in the summer and turns brown in the winter.

Toward the edge of the desert, a rare **scimitar-horned oryx** finds a rich area of grass. These migrant mammals live in the southern Sahara when the rains are due, and move south to find food when it's dry.

A combination of being overhunted and lack of food due to drought nearly made the addax antelope extinct at one time. They are still very rare, but their numbers are growing.

137

Living in herds of up to 100 animals, dorcas gazelles cross huge distances of open desert to find food. They can go for months without **drinking**, getting all their water from plants. The lushest plants grow at the edges of the desert.

Both male and female dorcas gazelles have horns. Those of females are thin and straight, but the males' curve backward and point up at the ends.

When startled, a dorcas calls through its nose to warn the herd. The call sounds like a duck quacking.

If a predator strikes the herd, the gazelles **run away** at speeds of up to **55 mph** (90 kph).

Head to head

Male dorcas gazelles guard their territories fiercely, marking out areas with piles of dung and tussling with other males who overstep the mark. They also lock horns over potential mates. Females don't fight.

The smallest species of gazelle has the longest legs in relation to the size of its body—great for sprinting away from predators!

139

Like most desert animals, the rodents are foraging for food before the day gets too hot, when they head off to their burrows under ground. Small animals heat up quickly in the hot sun and lose body water if they are not in the shade.

Patrolling the desert skies, the golden eagle is a major predator of rodents, along with desert eagle owls and the rare Houbara bustards.

Gerbils have excellent hearing, which they use to detect predators and also to find mates. Being so small in such a vast desert, it can be hard for gerbils to locate each other.

There's danger flying overhead.

Watch out!

Run, rodent, run!

9:09 am The nocturnal jerboa is finishing a night's foraging when it is disturbed by an eagle-eyed predator.

Of the 22 species of rodent living in the Sahara, half are gerbils.

Just as a camel stores fat in its hump, the **fat-tailed gerbil** carries its reserves in its club-shaped tail. Like many rodents, these gerbils have scent glands on their stomachs and mark their territories by rubbing their stomachs on the ground.

The fat-tailed gerbil eats insects, which it routs out from the ground with its pointed snout.

By far the biggest living thing on this page is the **euphorbia** plant, which can grow up to 10 ft (3 m) tall. The succulent plant takes in water when it rains and stores it in its leaves to survive dry periods.

The jerboa's name comes from the Arabic word *yerbo*, which means "big thighs." The jerboa also has a tail longer than its body, which acts as a prop when it sits still.

9:10 am With a leap of its huge legs, the jerboa springs into action and bounds away from the eagle.

9:10 am Despite being just 4 in (12 cm) long, the jerboa can leap up to 6 ft (2 m) in one jump, taking it safely to its burrow in a matter of moments. Made it!

The hind legs are four times bigger than the front legs.

The jerboa will spend the rest of the day asleep.

1 Desert shrub *Commosum calligonum*

A sudden wind appears and parts of the desert become a sandstorm as the fine, dusty sand is blown everywhere. Some winds gradually blow themselves out, but others stop as abruptly as this one has arrived.

Although some distance away, the **fennec fox** is woken by the sandstorm. Keeping its ears flat, it picks up the sound of the swirling winds.

The **horned viper** stays in its daytime bed, away from the sandstorm that could easily bury it. Its burrow was once made and occupied by a gerbil.

Away from the storm, the **agama** continues sunbathing. As the reptile warms up, it changes color from brown to blue and red.

The **dorcas gazelle** is caught unaware by the sandstorm. Sometimes hot air and lots of flies are blown in ahead of the storm, giving a warning.

Too big to hide, the **camel** keeps the sand at bay by closing its nostrils. It has extralong eyelashes and a third eyelid to protect its eyes.

Cold-blooded reptiles need to warm up before they start their day. They can stand the heat long after mammals have headed for shade, but will also take shelter when it gets too hot in summer.

A **chameleon** searches for insects to eat, its eyes able to swivel in different directions as it slowly paces the desert. It is not disturbed by the hot sand under its feet, even though it is more used to living in trees. Its split feet are ideal for gripping branches.

Desert monitors are the **biggest** reptiles in the Sahara. They swallow

The monitor's diet includes snakes and lizards—even those of the same species.

Agamas eat anything, from flowers to grasshoppers. This **desert agama** has wrestled with a scorpion, able to avoid its sting. But perhaps even more amazing is the agamas' trick of eating flies, which they catch in midflight by jumping into the air.

A skink's long, thin toes and pointed face are ideal tools for digging in the sand. The skink is also known as the sand fish because it moves around by swimming through the sand, hunting down insects found below the surface.

Desert monitors hibernate during the winter in shallow burrows that are not much bigger than themselves. They also burrow to avoid the strong summer sun around midday. If they get too hot, they die.

their prey whole.

Common agamas inhabit rocky areas, rather than the hot dunes. They live in small groups, but it is easy to spot the leader: he's the brightly colored male among the brown females.

Going, going, gone...

11:01 am While swimming for insects in the sand, the skink spies a predatory monitor lizard in the distance.

11:01 am Without hesitation, the skink takes a dive into the sand. Scales cover its ears to stop them from filling with sand.

11:02 am Seconds later the skink is well hidden, although it keeps a wary eye out for the danger to pass.

At one time, ostriches lived in the wild in the Sahara. Now they live in the Sahel, the semidesert just south of the Sahara. It is a sign that the dry desert is spreading.

To preen or scratch, an ostrich can bend and twist its head right down to its feet.

Who needs to fly?

Ostriches cannot fly, but they are the fastest animals on two legs, reaching speeds of 45 mph (70 kph) for 30 minutes at a time. Should a predator catch one, it will receive a nasty kick from the powerful bird.

Ostriches are herd animals, but they do not just stick to their own kind. They often graze alongside herds of antelopes.

Ostriches are not just record-breaking runners; they are also the world's biggest and heaviest birds. They also lay the largest eggs, around 7 in (18 cm) long.

Laying all their eggs in one basket

12:30 pm At night, the male ostrich stands guard in a shared nest, sitting on the clutch of 40–50 eggs.

40 days later The chicks begin to hatch. Only half the eggs will have survived to bear chicks.

The chicks are already 1 ft (30 cm) tall at birth. Within a month, they can run with their parents.

This egg is **life-size**.

One ostrich egg is equivalent to 24 chicken eggs—a good meal for predators such as this **Egyptian vulture**. The bird throws stones at the egg to smash its shell.

Caterpillar take-away

1:00 pm In one of their foraging expeditions, the ants sniff out the remains of a caterpillar. Within moments the whole troop is upon it.

The Sun is

blazing, the summer heat is unbearable, but down among the sand grains there is still plenty of activity. Worker ants are out and about in the endless search for food for their queen.

1:10 pm The ants load up with chunks of grub and head back to the nest. By now the temperature is so hot, some ants will burn and not make it back.

Ants have two eyes and three sensory organs in their forehead. These extra "eyes" don't register images, but they can see light patterns, which the ants use to find their way across the sand.

There are 66 species of ant in the Sahara. Most live in underground nests, where there is some moisture, but some live in trees or near oases. Others inhabit dry dunes and rocks. Those that live underground are seed-eaters, carrying food to their nest in their jaws.

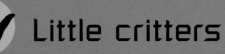

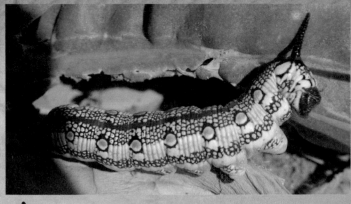

Sphinx moth caterpillars are also called hornworms because they have a horn on one end. The horn is harmless.

A **sphinx moth caterpillar** munches on euphorbia leaves, eating nonstop until it is ready to change into a moth. It was born in the tree so it could start eating straight after hatching.

Teams of **dung** beetles gather mammal dung and roll it home.

The tiny **seed bug** lives in many parts of the world. It hibernates during cold winters, but comes out to sunbathe when the weather is warmer. It feeds on plant seeds: at just ½ in (1 cm) long, an animal this small can eat only tiny portions.

Dung beetles may have an unsavory choice of habitat, but they make good use of their resources. They not only feed on the dung they collect from the desert mammals, but also lay their eggs in it.

1 Camel

Early afternoon is the hottest part of the day in the Saharan summer. There is very little action; those animals too big to hide from the heat underground seek out what limited shade the desert can offer.

The **fennec fox** has swapped its daytime burrow for a shady tree, its fur reflecting the heat. It even has furry feet so it can walk on hot sand.

Hidden under a rock, the **horned viper** faces a threat. It coils up and rubs its scales to make a warning sound; if that fails, it bares its fangs.

The **agama** is one of the few active animals, seeking out a mate. He has warmed up to full color, but the female remains brown all day.

The **dorcas gazelle** is conserving energy in the shade. Without this rest, it would not be able to live on the limited water it gets from its food.

Camels keep active for most of the day, so this baby takes advantage of the heat break to drink from its mother. It's also sheltered under there!

After rain millions of desert locusts may group together to form a swarm. Swept along by winds, these locusts will eat nearly every plant in their path.

Locusts that like to keep away from other locusts are called solitary.

Swarming locusts give off a special chemical that attracts other locusts.

The solitary (nonswarming) locust looks and behaves like a grasshopper. It flies by night.

Crowd behavior

When locusts crowd together, they change into gregarious or swarming locusts after four hours. They also change color.

The gregarious locust is pink at first and then becomes yellow when it is fully grown.

Desert locusts have been a serious pest since agriculture began.

Serious eaters

Each locust will eat its own weight in food each day. A swarm containing millions of insects can destroy crops and help to create famine.

153

Ponds and oases are the best

places to see the variety of birds in the desert. Sandgrouse, desert larks, and wheatears are common locals; storks and swallows may be migrant visitors, while eagle owls and hawks are roving hunters.

White storks use thermals of hot air to help carry them across the desert.

A long way to go

Migrating birds are often seen crossing the desert. Among the largest are the white storks that leave Europe in the fall and fly over the Sahara to reach southern Africa for the winter.

Sandgrouse are found all over the desert, and will fly long distances to find water to drink.

Water transporter

These chestnut-bellied sandgrouse are well camouflaged against sand and vegetation. They fly in flocks to watering holes at dawn and dusk, where they drink and also soak up water in their soft breast feathers to take back to their chicks.

Desert eagle owls hunt rodents such as jerboas and gerbils, and even other birds.

Silent killer

The desert eagle owl's wings are designed for silent flight, making it a very effective hunter. Flying low over the ground, the owl is ready to pounce on an unsuspecting victim.

Only adult male **wheatears** have this dazzling white crown.

Sandgrouse are usually found in **flocks** of about **60 birds**.

1 Palm trees   2 Fennec fox burrow

With sunset comes cooler temperatures, bringing a burst of activity to the desert. Diurnal, or daytime, animals come out of the shade to hunt for supper, while the nocturnal ones are waking up for the night.

The **fennec fox** emerges from its burrow, ready to start hunting. It is careful to look and listen for predators such as eagles and hawks.

Just becoming active, the **horned viper** side-winds across the sand. It moves its body quickly, one part at a time, so it has less contact with the hot sand.

Just becoming active, the

The hungry **agama** polishes off an evening meal of a small gecko. This is a large meal: it mostly feeds on insects such as ants and locusts.

During the hot summer months, the **dorcas gazelle** continues to rest until nightfall. It scrapes the sand with its hooves to make a smooth bed.

Resuming its journey across the open sand, the **camel** looks for grazing places. It will munch for several hours on any shrubs it may find.

Camels are often called ships of the desert because they are so well designed for life in a dry environment and can easily carry heavy loads.

A baby camel stays with its mother for two to three years.

Captive camels

There are almost no wild (or feral) camels left in the Sahara—only domesticated ones. They are well cared for, and taken to wells to drink and to grazing areas to replenish their fat stores.

Ready, set, up!

1 A camel rests with its legs tucked under its body.

2 The camel rises by first getting into a kneeling position.

3 Then the camel pushes up with its back legs.

4 Finally, the camel straightens out its front legs.

5 The camel is up on all fours and ready to go.

If a camel's hump leans to one side, it has used up its fat reserves.

A male camel gets very defensive during the mating season.

Best foot forward
Camels' feet are ideal for crossing the dunes. Each foot is split into two pads that do not sink into the sand nor slip on flat rocks. The soft pads also act like shock absorbers.

Under cover of darkness, when it is much cooler, a cheetah prowls around looking for a meal. Moving in, a pair of golden jackals waits to scavenge the cheetah's kill—if it's been lucky enough to find any prey.

The cheetah uses its tail for balance and can make sharp turns when chasing after gazelles.

Big canine teeth enable the cheetah to bite its prey on the neck, causing it to suffocate. It then gobbles its meal in case a hyena attacks.

Fastest feet on Earth

Cheetahs hunt either by stalking their prey to catch it unawares or by sprinting after it at high speeds. They are the fastest of all land animals, reaching 60 mph (100 kph)—but only for short distances.

Running at 55 mph (90 kph) the cheetah will be taking an incredible three and a half strides per second.

A changing menu throughout the night

In the cool of the early morning, **dorcas gazelles** are easy prey, especially those too young and small to run with the herd.

Cape hares are nocturnal targets. They can put up a good chase, making sudden turns, and leaping up to 12 ft (4 m) in one bound.

Sniffing around a carcass, a golden jackal is looking for parts of the prey that other scavengers have left behind. Its mate is nearby, and together they will take home food for their young by regurgitating what they have eaten and feeding it to the pups.

161

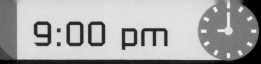

Look out small rodents,

mammals, and birds because on warm nights the snakes come out looking for a meal. The horned viper and its close relative the sand viper may cover a large area on their hunt. They will leave zigzag tracks in the sand.

Disappearing act

The sand viper shuffles down into the sand by rocking its body from side to side. It shovels sand over itself as it submerges. This squat snake will soon be almost completely hidden and ready to strike an unsuspecting victim.

Snakes can sense vibrations in the air, so the slightest movement from other animals can reveal the location of potential prey.

The sand viper's light, mottled skin makes it hard to spot against sand. The waterproof skin helps the snake retain moisture in the desert heat.

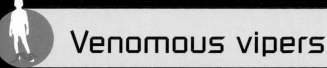
Biting off more than you can chew

8:29 pm The horned viper has killed a bird by injecting venom into it. Now it has to eat it!

As the horned viper lies ready to ambush its prey, all that can be seen are its thornlike horns and catlike eyes. It will attack with an open mouth and stab the animal with its long fangs.

8:37 pm Like all snakes, the horned viper can dislocate its jaws, allowing it to swallow prey wider than itself. Nearly half the bird is now inside.

8:47 pm Ten minutes later, the bird is passing slowly down the snake. It will take several weeks for it to be digested.

Slither, slide, strike...
In the enveloping darkness the sand viper is out hunting. Its fangs are folded back into its mouth and will only be dropped down for biting.

1 Desert eagle owl

Night brings cool air to the desert. In winter, the temperature can fall to below freezing, yet many desert animals are active at night. It is much easier for furry mammals to keep warm at night than cool in the day.

The **fennec fox** senses prey, hearing the slightest movement with its huge ears. It also has good night vision for spotting larger animals.

The **horned viper** hides underground to ambush unsuspecting prey. It lunges, bites, and kills with the poison stored in venom sacs near its fangs.

As the air cools, the **agama** fades back to its less colorful skin. It will spend the night with its family group, hidden among the desert rocks.

Dorcas gazelles are diurnal, but in very hot weather they are active during the night. If rain has fallen, a large herd gathers to feed on plants.

The **camel** has a thick wool coat to keep it warm during the cold night. In summer, when the coat molts, the camel stores heat from the day.

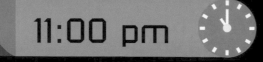

On the alert, the sand cat looks around carefully before leaving the safety of its burrow to hunt. It can travel as much as 5 miles (8 km) in a single night, searching for prey by walking and listening.

When threatened, sand cats will crouch beside a small rock or tuft of grass. One of the pair pictured here is looking as fierce as it can.

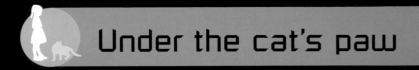
It's snake for supper

A sand cat will attack a poisonous snake. This one is about to whack a horned viper over the head with its paw. It will then bite through the snake's neck to kill it.

Pounce, kill, play...

5:02 pm Crouching low, a sand cat waits beside a jerboa's burrow. It may return to the burrow at night hoping to catch one of the occupants.

11:36 pm In the cool of the night a jerboa is out looking for food. A sand cat is about to pounce and will kill it with a quick bite through its neck.

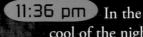

6:22 am The sand cat plays with the dead jerboa before munching it. Water from the body gives the sand cat the moisture it needs.

A female fennec fox stays home with her young cubs while the male goes out hunting. It takes little time for these expert diggers to create their underground dens. They are kept very clean and neat, and provide a safe and cool daytime retreat.

Just popping out for a meal

6.00 pm As dusk falls and the air begins to cool, the foxes wake up and the male emerges.

6.05 pm After a quick check for predators, the male starts to look for food to take back to the female in the den.

7.00 am The fox makes one last hunt before it gets hot. He may stay out of his den during the day, returning tonight.

What big ears they have.... All the better for hearing insect prey, even underground. The large surface also helps give off body heat.

Between a rock and a hard place

Out in the open, the foxes face predators such as birds of prey. Their pale, sandy-colored fur provides some camouflage, but it is safer to hide inside a cave or in crevice among the rocks.

The foxes' diet includes moisture-rich plants, eggs, and birds such as the sandgrouse...

... And any animal small enough for them to catch. Lizards and desert locusts make a crunchy snack!

Small rodents, such as gerbils, are pounced on much like a cat catches mice.

Feeding the family

Fennec fox cubs feed on their mother's milk until they are one month old. Once they are weaned, the male will stop bringing the female food and she leaves the den to hunt for herself.

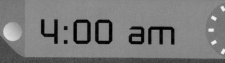
Scorpions are probably the oldest stinging things in existence. They stay hidden under rocks or in burrows during the day and come out at night to hunt—as does the fast-moving camel spider.

Multiple birth

Scorpions give birth to up to 100 live young. The newborn scorpions climb up their mother's legs and onto her back. They stay there until their first molt a few days after their birth.

The babies get a ride until they can fend for themselves.

The yellow scorpion has the strongest venom of all scorpions and is very quick to sting. The pincers are used to hold prey.

The Sting is as sharp as a needle.

Venom-injecting sting at the end of the tail.

Deadly injection

The scorpion has pushed its tail downward to pierce the skin of the gecko and inject its deadly venom. It now holds the gecko in its pincers and starts to tuck in. It won't need to eat for a while after this feast.

Shedding its skin

A young scorpion sheds its skin in a safe hiding place. Before molting, its blood pressure increases, making the old skeleton crack. Scorpions usually molt six times before they are adult.

Camel spiders can give a nasty bite. They have very strong jaws for their size.

When it has molted, the scorpion is soft-bodied and needs to hide until its new skeleton has hardened.

Looking like a big hairy spider, this strange beast known as a camel spider is actually neither spider nor scorpion. A fast mover—it can reach 10 mph (16 kph)—it feeds on insects, lizards, small mammals, and birds.

Mountain

The Andes of South America is the longest mountain range in the world. Some of its creatures live in forests, some in lakes, some in grasslands, and some on rocky slopes. Explore their exciting world over 24 hours.

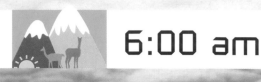

1 Guanaco

A lone guanaco stands

in the cold morning air, watching the Sun rise over the Andes. By the time the Sun has emerged over the mountain peaks, the sunrise can seem later than it actually is.

A herd of **vicuñas** makes its way down from its sleeping area high up in the mountains. The lower slopes provide lusher grass for grazing.

Spectacled bears are most active at dawn and dusk, heading up the slopes to the grasslands to feed on their favorite food: puya plants.

The nocturnal **culpeo** breakfasts on a carcass. It usually hunts small animals such as rodents and lizards, but is happy to scavenge a free meal.

Before **Andean condors** take flight in the morning they stretch out their wings to dry their feathers, which are wet with dawn dew.

A **puma** sniffs the air, picking up the scent of another puma's urine. Curling its lips makes its sense of smell more sensitive.

The plants of the paramo—

many of which don't grow anywhere else—attract lots of birds, which feed on their nectar and the insects that pollinate them.

Hummingbirds like to feed from the 40 ft- (12 m-) tall *Puya ramondii* herb.

Andean hillstars, like other hummingbirds, survive the cold nights by going into torpor—they lower their body temperatures to one-third of their daytime level to save energy.

Andean flickers are woodpeckers—birds that are most famous for hammering their bills into tree trunks. But there are no trees on the paramo, only shrubs and smaller plants, so the flicker picks insects off the rocks to eat.

Bearded helmetcrest hummingbirds prefer walking to flying in their search for food, since they eat insects rather than nectar. The bird gets its name from the crest that makes its head appear twice its real size!

Caracaras are small birds of prey. They patrol the paramo in groups, looking for carcasses to scavenge and also eating insects and snails.

Part of the parrot family, **rufous-fronted parakeets** are an endangered species. They live only on the lower slopes of the paramo—areas that are threatened by overgrazing and farming.

Seedsnipes don't build nests, but dig shallow scrapes on the ground where they lay their eggs, which they sit on for about four weeks until they hatch. The chicks are able to walk and eat right away.

177

To the south of the paramo, an Andean hairy armadillo wanders over the barren puna. Sniffing out an **insect**, it unearths the food with a scrape of its long, sharp claws.

Twenty bony plates cover the armadillo's body. Hair grows between the plates, keeping the animal warm.

On the menu

Armadillos are omnivores: they'll eat anything from plants to rodents.

Insects such as beetles are nourishing snacks, but they are not very filling.

Armadillos will dig under and even into rotting carcasses to get at juicy maggots.

The armadillo is only active in the daytime during winter. Summer heat forces it to turn its day around, searching for food at night and spending the day in cool burrows.

Armadillos live alone, only sharing burrows with their young. ....

The word "armadillo" means little plated one.

Strong claws make fast work of digging a 10 ft- (3 m-) deep burrow. The holes are only used once.

The best place to hide from predators is underground, but when there's no burrow to dive into the armadillo covers its legs and relies on its armor plating.

179

1 Juvenile Andean condor
2 Adult male Andean condor

Just as there are high peaks in mountainous territory, there are also deep valleys. Colca Canyon is thought to be the world's deepest gorge (narrow valley). The steep slopes are a favored roosting site for Andean condors.

Vicuñas are grazers: their days are taken up with eating, drinking, and chewing the cud. Young vicuñas even eat while lying down.

Spectacled bears live in cloud forests below the grasslands. During the day, they rest in the trees, bending branches to make "nests" to sit in.

Fully fed, the nocturnal **culpeo** settles down to rest among the rocks. An adult culpeo has few predators, so it is safe for it to sleep out in the open.

An **Andean condor** finds a dead vicuña: this will be its first meal for days. Its strong, hooked bill easily tears through the decaying flesh.

Solitary **pumas** spend the daytime asleep. Only mothers with young cubs are still out hunting to keep their offspring well fed.

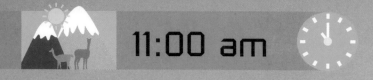
There's competition in the air between the birds of prey that live around the Andes. Scavenging turkey vultures sniffing out a carcass are sometimes followed by condors, which chase them off the food.

The condor's large wingspan allows it to glide for hundreds of miles (kilometers).

All birds rely on their feathers for flight. They cannot fly if feathers are bent or damaged.

Turkey vultures have weak **claws** because they do not need to kill for food.

Turkey vultures are the only birds with a good sense of smell, which is useful for tracking down dead animals through tall grasses and shrubs.

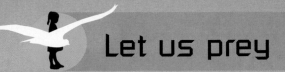

Condors have excellent eyesight, able to see dead animals and even birds' eggs on the ground while soaring high above them. They fly 200 miles (320 km) a day looking for food.

With an outstretched neck that makes him stand up straight, a male condor raises his wings in a courtship display, trying to attract a mate. The bird hisses and clucks for female attention.

••••••The condor rides air currents to gain height. It rises over half a mile (1 km) in just two minutes.

A flying start

11:30 am Peregrine falcons lay their eggs in a shallow nest, called a scrape, right on the edge of the mountainside.

You need to be quick to spot a **peregrine falcon**: they are among the world's fastest birds. They can reach 145 mph (230 km/h) diving for prey, which they kill with their sharp bills.

30 days later The chicks have hatched, and just seven weeks later they will learn to fly—a dangerous task at the top of a mountain.

4 months later The chicks have survived flying lessons, but still rely on both parents to bring them food: other birds.

Condors are scavengers:

they feed on animals that are already **dead**, but they might also attack young or dying animals. Despite feeding in **flocks**, it can take them days to finish a large carcass.

Bald head for poking inside carcass without getting feathers dirty.

Sharp, hooked bill for gripping prey and ripping into flesh.

The big feast

First come, first served

The birds gather around the day's meal in a strict pecking order. Males eat first; they are bigger than the females and perform displays to frighten off other scavengers that might be around. They rarely fight, because that could damage their feathers.

Having gorged itself on guanaco, this young **condor** waits for a thermal (air current) to carry it into flight. It has eaten too much to take off itself.

The flock COVERS the carcass.

185

Herds of grazing

guanacos are a familar sight across the Andean slopes, especially browsing plants on the puna grasslands. There are four species of South American camelid: guanacos and vicuñas are wild, but llamas and alpacas are farmed.

On the dry grasslands, guanacos keep themselves clean not with water, but by rolling in a dust bath.

Most herds are family groups of one male leading lots of females and their young, which are called crias. Young males without mates form herds of their own; older males wander the mountains alone.

Guanacos chew their food by grinding it against their hard gums.

Like all camelid species, **vicuñas** have the ability to run fast—which could mean the difference between life and death on the grasslands, where there is nowhere to hide from predators.

Alpacas have the softest, curliest wool of all the camelid species, especially on the crias (baby llamas or alpacas).

Llamas are among the most common animals in the Andes. They are domesticated guanacos, farmed for their wool.

Guanacos can go without drinking for long periods, getting all their **water** from food.

Crias start life with a bump, since their mothers give birth standing up. After a year with Mom, male crias are kicked out of the herd by the leader, who does not want any competition for the females.

Like all quadrupeds, a cria is born front feet first, breaking its fall. It will start to walk just one hour later.

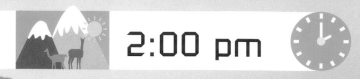

1 Guanaco

Between the peaks, lakes dot the Altiplano region of the Andes. Some are filled with rain or melted snow; others form from geysers that erupt from below the surface. Many provide drinking water for animals.

Two young **vicuñas** start a play-fight, imitating the adults in the herd. Adult males wrestle each other to take sole control of the herd's females.

Feeling hungry, the **spectacled bear** surveys the forest for a snack. There are plenty of bromeliad plants within arm's reach of its nest.

Young **culpcos** are targets for birds of prey, so the safest place for them to sleep during the day is in an underground burrow with their mother.

The **Andean condor** gets messy when it feeds, and needs to preen its feathers afterward. It even rubs its head on the ground to get the blood off.

A female **puma** watches over her three cubs while at rest. The small, young cubs could be targeted as prey by foxes or even other pumas.

There are 41 islands in Lake Titicaca, which is nearly twice the size of Delaware.

The freshwater Lake Titicaca is the world's highest navigable lake (big enough for boats to sail on). Located in the Altiplano, it is home to frogs and fish that don't exist anywhere else in the world.

The Titicaca frog's saggy skin helps it to breathe. Frogs absorb oxygen through their skin, and the bigger the skin, the more oxygen it can absorb.

This is the world's largest frog.

The giant Titicaca frog lives in the shallows of the lake, and keeps from roasting in the sun by never leaving the water. Its dark skin also gives protection against the Sun's rays.

Some Titicaca frogs have green skin; others can be dark and spotted.

Teams of **neotropic cormorants** work together to get food. They wade through the lake, flapping their wings to chase the fish into shallow water.

The lake teems with **fish,** which **attract** lots of birds.

Argentine silverside fish

Killifish

The **puna ibis** uses its long, curved bill to probe for food in the shallow waters and the mud around the edge of the lake. Groups of ibis feed together, seeking fish, frogs, and small aquatic animals to eat.

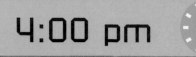
At the start of the rainy season, flocks of flamingos settle on the **salt lakes** in the Altiplano. The lakes are far smaller than Lake Titicaca, yet **thousands** of birds feed here.

Three's a crowd

Three species of flamingos live on the lakes: Andean, Chilean, and Puna. As soon as the birds arrive, they start the search for a mate.

There's no competition between the three species as they eat different food.

Flamingos turn pink from the carotenoids in the algae or shrimp they eat. It's the same pigment that turns carrots orange.

192

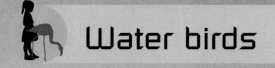

Bringing up baby

October Flamingo pairs build their nests, ready for laying a single egg. The lakeside is covered in volcano-shaped mounds of mud.

December The fluffy gray chick has just hatched. The 2 ft- (60 cm-) high nest keeps the bird safe from any flood waters.

April The chick has grown out of its "baby" feathers and is ready to fly, but still relies on its mother for food.

At night, flamingos roost near hot geysers to keep warm.

Flamingos turn their heads upside-down to eat. They use their bills as sieves, sifting food from the water.

There's more to the Altiplano than lakes and puna grassland. The Andes are a chain of volcanoes, many of which are still bubbling away underground. This activity comes to the surface through geysers and pools of boiling mud.

An outgoing geyser

The hot steam cools in the air, condenses into water, and runs into lakes.

4:00 pm The pressure of volcanic activity pushes steam through holes in the ground, making the water in the geyser boil.

Bubbling mud might not look as dramatic as a geyser, but it has an equally strong presence: the mud is full of sulfur, a mineral that makes the air stink like rotten eggs.

4:01 pm The steam quickly cools and becomes water. Only bacteria and algae can live in the boiling pool, coloring it red and green.

6:10 am As the pressure builds up below ground, the geyser suddenly and briefly erupts, sending a jet of hot water and steam into the air.

Hot days, freezing nights, strong winds, and very little rainfall turns parts of the Altiplano into salt deserts. The salts are minerals found in the ground, brought to the surface in lakes.

Melted snow and water from geysers run down the slopes to form lakes.

Small **iguanid lizards** scamper over the lake's salty crust, catching flies to eat.

195

1 Guanaco

Sunset falls later in the day the farther south you move through the Andes, away from the equator. With light fading as soon as the Sun sinks behind the peaks, there is little time for a guanaco to find a safe place to sleep.

Unlike guanacos, **vicuñas** drink lots of water during the day. They never stray far from rivers or lakes when grazing on the rocky slopes.

The **spectacled bear** leaves its tree to search the forest and paramo for food. Although mostly vegetarian, it will also eat small animals.

The **culpeo** rouses itself from its daytime rest to go hunting. A male culpeo with young cubs needs to get food for his family as well as himself.

Feeding and preening all day must be tiring work for an **Andean condor**! Giving a huge yawn, it prepares to return to its roost for the night.

From a high point on the peaks, the **puma** scans the mountains for prey. It prefers large deer or guanaco, but any meat will do.

With its thick fur, grooming is an important part of viscacha hair care! ....

Viscachas have many predators,

Perched on a rock, a male viscacha watches for predators while his colony feeds. At the first sign of danger, he will call out a warning.

A young viscacha stirs from sunbathing with a big stretch. It's time to find food, which young viscachas are able to eat as soon as they are born.

A viscacha's view

A day in the life

8:15 am Much of the viscacha's day is spent sunbathing. Exposing its belly to the sunshine, the animal soon warms up after a cold night.

5:30 pm Dusk is the rodent's busiest time, scouring the puna for food. It will eat any plants it finds, including grass and moss.

7:00 pm As night falls, the viscacha heads off to a safe burrow to sleep.

Although they look like rabbits, viscachas are "cousins" of chinchillas.

The big cats of the Andes are proof that size is not important. Pampas cats and Geoffroy's cats are about the same size as domestic cats—but they are fierce predators. Yet they are rarely seen in the wild, hiding in trees in the forests on the lower slopes or among scrub higher up the mountain.

 Learning through play, **Pampas kittens** practice their climbing and observation skills—tools they need to be successful hunters.

An adult Pampas cat looks stocky, but its big legs are actually thick with fur. Some Pampas cats have pale fur; others have bold stripes.

Catty behavior

Geoffroy's cats, like many wild cats, have similar habits to pet cats—such as washing with their paws.

The cats are expert climbers at the age of six weeks, scrambling out of the rocky dens where they were born.

A startled cat gives a defensive yowl to protect its mate. If threatened, the aggressive animal will spit and bite.

Patterned fur **camouflages** the cats so they can hunt unseen.

In a land of predators, the puma is king of the carnivores. It is the largest cat of the high Andes, yet it is rarely heard: it doesn't roar, but has a call that sounds like a human scream.

A close encounter

Pumas only spend time with others during mating, or as young cubs with their mothers. The cubs' spotted fur grows out as they become adults.

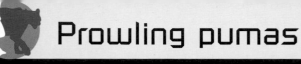

Keeping a low profile

The puma's hunting technique is all about surprise. It stays low to the ground, silently stalking the prey, then suddenly springs up and kills its victim with a single, ferocious bite.

A long wait for dinner

7:15 pm A female puma kills a guanaco she has been tracking since dusk. She hunts all day to feed her cubs; now it's time to find food for herself.

7:20 pm There are too many scavengers around for her to eat undisturbed, so the puma drags the carcass into shrubs to hide it until later.

10:00 pm Now that it is dark, the puma finally tucks in. Even though the cubs have eaten during the day, they can't resist a nibble!

1 Spectacled bear

Night is **a** dangerous time for smaller animals because the darkness brings out some ferocious predators. Pumas and great horned owls can snatch a deer or rodent without warning, while culpeos are expert egg thieves.

The **vicuñas** have headed back up the slope to their sleeping area just beneath the snowline. They will sleep among the rocks until daybreak.

The **spectacled bear** wanders high into the paramo in its search for food. Mountain climbing is as easy as scaling a tree for this agile animal.

Young male **culpeos** need to establish their own hunting grounds. Sniffing scent markings tells them if the territory has already been taken.

Mateless **Andean condors** roost in groups at night. There are no nesting materials this high up in the mountains so the nest is a bare ledge.

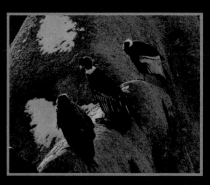

The **puma** returns to the prey it buried earlier. It waits until nighttime to eat, when there are fewer scavengers around to compete for the food.

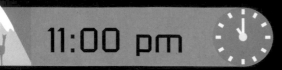
Named after the white markings on its face, the spectacled bear actually has excellent eyesight.

Since leaving its daytime nest at sunset, the spectacled bear has been foraging in its cloud forest home and up on the paramo. It is more active at night than in the day.

Big bear, small threat
South America's only bear species, the spectacled bear is one of the largest mammals in the Andes. It mostly eats plants, but occasionally tops off its diet with small animals such as rodents.

Despite their size, these bears are very agile. They have no problem shinnying up trees or stretching up to the branches for a tasty bromeliad plant.

It's twins!

Female bears give birth to two or three tiny cubs that are no bigger than kittens. Home is a den on the forest floor, hidden among rocks or tree roots.

Young cubs can learn essential skills together. A brotherly tussle is good training for adult fighting.

Sharp **Claws** are essential tools for tree climbers.

After the age of one year, spectacled bears live alone. They are very timid and are rarely seen.

Swooping

in on an unwary chinchilla, a great horned owl grabs the prey in its talons, killing it instantly. The owl's success is helped by its silent flight.

After eating, owls cough up pellets of the bits of food they do not digest, such as fur and bones.

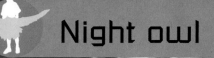
Soft, loose feathers muffle the sound of flapping wings.

It makes sense
The owl has excellent vision and can see in daylight, but even better at night. It also uses its extraordinary hearing to help it hunt in the dark.

These large tufts are not ears but feathery "horns" that give the owl its name.

Feeding on demand
Great horned owls watch for prey from mountain perches, or while gliding near to the ground. The prey is caught in moments, and the owl rips into it with its bill. Smaller prey is swallowed whole.

The owl's eyes are huge compared to its face. If human eyes were similar, they'd be as big as oranges!

The owl's diet includes rodents, fish, and even other birds, which it plucks before eating.

Small animals such as rodents lose heat easily, but the chinchilla braves the freezing night air wrapped in its own fur coat. Each follicle has 60 soft hairs growing from it, making the fur very thick.

A chinchilla has a built-in defense against predators: it molts easily, leaving attackers with a mouthful of fur, not animal. However, this doesn't always work...

The chinchilla's whiskers, or vibrissae, act as an extra pair of eyes at night, when the animal feels its way around in the dark.

Just chin-chillin'

It's been a busy day...

7:00 am Sunning themselves at dawn to get warm and dry, chinchillas start the day with a roll in a dust bath to clean their fur.

3:30 pm Resting in a den among the rocks, a female feeds her kit. Born with a full fur coat, the kit can also eat plants right from birth.

8:00 pm It's time to get back outside to find food, which chinchillas hold in their paws to eat.

Chinchillas are not the only rodents out at night: they share the puna with **montane guinea pigs**. These wild animals are the cousins of the domestic guinea pigs kept as pets all over the world.

Wild guinea pigs live underground in burrows. Their pointed faces are ideally shaped for pushing through tunnels and also for foraging for plants to eat.

Having light-colored fur is good camouflage for a chinchilla on the rocks.

Guinea pigs live for about four years in the wild.

211

Arctic

Welcome to the Arctic—the icy, remote

land at the very top of the world. Did you know that most of it is just
a big frozen sea, with a few fringes of land around the edges?

1 Harp seal pup

At dawn, the short night begins to lift. At this time of year nights are dusky but never really dark, because the Sun doesn't set completely. All by himself on the shadowy ice, a harp seal pup lies resting and waiting for his mother to deliver his next meal.

Using his keen sense of smell, a **polar bear** stalks prey. If there's a seal breathing hole nearby, he has a good chance of catching his supper.

There's nothing like a horny hoof and a big pair of antlers when a **caribou** needs to scratch himself in hard-to-reach places.

This **Arctic fox** is tucking into the carcass of a bird he has killed. If he can't eat it all, he will bury it in the snow in case he can come back.

To pull his huge body out of the water and onto an ice floe, this basking **walrus** uses his long pointed tusks as levers.

Unlike other owls, **snowies** don't sleep in the day and hunt at night. They can set out to find prey at almost any time.

Plentiful in Arctic seas,

harp seals are hugely sociable, living and traveling together in big, noisy groups. They **gather** on floating ice floes far from shore and **dive** for small fish in deep water. Harp-seal pups, born in late **winter**, are still very young in April.

Mother harp seals touch noses with their pups as a greeting, and to identify them as their own.

Because of their pale fur, new babies are called "whitecoats."

When they're first born, pups feed on their mom's rich milk. Soon they have a thick layer of blubber to keep them warm.

Two female seals both think this young pup is their own. If they can't work things out, there's likely to be a fight.

These two are still youngsters, but their white fur has fallen out and a thinner, gray, adult coat has taken its place.

Ice, ice babies

Just before giving birth (called whelping), female harp seals haul themselves onto winter pack ice in their thousands. An area of ice where pups are born and nursed by their mothers is called a whelping patch.

For their first two weeks, pups just lie on the ice and wait for their moms to come and feed them. Their thick white fur keeps them warm.

Many Arctic animals are white so they can't be seen in the snow. This natural disguise, called camouflage, conceals some creatures from predators and allows others to attack before they're spotted by prey.

A male snowy owl is very hard to see against snow, ice, and pale, cloudy skies.

Ermines are a kind of stoat, and, like all stoats, they have a black tail tip, even when the rest of their fur is white. If hungry birds spot this, and swoop down to nip it, the ermine can pull away quickly.

Arctic wolves are closely related to ordinary gray wolves. One big difference, though, is their coloring—they are always pale. This snarling creature is almost pure white, but Arctic wolves are sometimes cream or light gray.

Look closely at this scene and you'll find a winter-white ptarmigan perched in the snow. In summer, this bird has speckled brown or gray feathers.

In addition to keeping him warm, the white fur coat on this baby seal makes it very hard for predators to spot him lying on the snow and ice.

Arctic hares are not just white in winter—they're white all year round, but in summer they have a slightly grayish hue. The biggest of all hares, they dig for food under the snow.

Bigger than an Arctic fox, an Arctic hare has huge feet, and can reach speeds of 40 mph (65 kph).

219

Except for humans, there are no animals in the Arctic that hunt polar bears. In addition to being the biggest bear in the world, this creature is the unchallenged ruler of the northern landscape.

Lone wanderer
With the exception of females with cubs, polar bears mostly live and hunt alone. They spend much of their lives on sea ice, hunting seals. Males are about twice as big as females; they weigh up to 1,400 lbs (650 kg)— as much as ten people.

Bear behavior

A polar bear's sense of smell is much better than yours or mine—he can sniff a seal from several miles (kilometers) away.

Home is where the hunt is

Polar bears live in areas where there is a mix of land ice, sea ice, and sea. In spring, males spend about a quarter of their time hunting. When they're not hunting, they're sleeping or resting.

These young males may look as if they're having a vicious battle. But, like many other animals, they just enjoying play fighting.

Like humans, polar bears walk on the soles of their feet, putting their heels down first.

With their warm fur and thick layer of blubber, polar bears get overheated very easily. Sometimes a rest is the best thing.

Female polar bears take care of their cubs until they're two or three years old—fathers aren't involved at all. Moms give birth (usually to two babies) in a den, and they don't come out until the cubs are several months old.

Safe at home

Cubs are born in the middle of winter, but they stay in their den until March or April. Before moms give birth, they have to store enough fat to nourish themselves for all that time, and to provide milk for their babies as well.

Watched by one of her babies, this mom enjoys being out in the open after her long months in the den.

Dens are usually in snow, but they can be dug out of snow-covered ground as well.

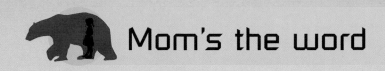
Life lessons

Cubs begin eating solid food as soon as Mom makes her first kill. After they're about a year old, they'll have learned to hunt from watching her.

Hungry birds such as gulls hang around for leftovers.

9:10 am Mom and her cubs eat and eat until they're stuffed. Nobody cares if they make a big mess.

9:50 am Phew! Three full bellies! Mom decides that breakfast time is over and calls her babies to join her in the water.

9:54 am Bears do most of their hunting on frozen bits of sea, so they're very good swimmers. Now they'll head home for a long nap.

Moms often make dens in big **snowdrifts** along the coast.

1 Walrus

The Arctic sky is very bright by 10:00 in the morning. A lone walrus, tired of sunning himself on an ice floe, lowers his body back into the sea. The visible splash is made by one of his back flippers, which propel him through the water.

Being able to break ice with his front paws is a very important hunting skill for a **polar bear.** Who knows? He might find food underneath.

There's still snow on the ground, so **reindeer** use their hooves and snouts to get at food underneath it. Mosses and lichens are particular favorites.

Male **Arctic foxes** usually hunt alone. They can cover huge distances—up to 600 miles (1,000 km)—in one trip looking for food.

Walruses are happy in water, and they're excellent swimmers. Like all his family, this one can stay submerged for up to half an hour.

Female **snowy owls** are a little bigger than males and flecked all over with brown. Males are mostly white with a few flecks on their chests and tails.

With their chubby cheeks and button noses, **walruses** look very cuddly. Big males are hard to cuddle, though—at 12 ft (3.5 m) long and 3,750 lbs (1,700 kg), they are the **size** of a small car.

Walruses are mammals, so they breathe air like we do. This one is swimming and breathing out at the same time.

Males love to bask together in the sun. This group has gathered on pack ice in the sea.

Walruses graze on the seabed for clams, sea cucumbers, and whelks. They live in shallow water so they can reach the surface to breathe.

Males (bulls) use their tusks for displays of aggression, even when they're not really fighting, and these can cause injury. Walruses are usually brown but they can turn quite pink in the sun.

Although they spend two-thirds of their lives in the water, walruses sometimes surface and rest on ice floes.

Under their wrinkly skin, walruses have a layer of fat (called **blubber**) about 4 in (10 cm) thick.

Feeding faces

Both male and female walruses have tusks and mustache whiskers. They use their snouts and their sensitive whiskers to feel for food on the ocean floor, then get at the food by squirting water from their mouths to loosen tasty morsels and digging them out with their snouts.

Lots of animals spend time under the sea. Even though it's freezing cold there, it's quite a bit warmer than the Arctic air, and there are lots of delicious fish to eat.

Narwhals are a type of small whale. The males have a single, straight tusk with spiral grooves along its length. Like a walrus tusk, this is actually a long tooth. Many historians think it inspired the myth of the unicorn.

In addition to swimming, walruses can also sleep underwater. To do this, they fill sacs in their throats with air. These act like floats, allowing the creatures to bob up and down while they snooze.

Pure white with smiley mouths, beluga whales have sharp teeth for eating fish and squid. Because they're small and a little slow, belugas are eaten by bigger whales—and even by polar bears.

Under the ice

Harp seal babies start to swim and catch fish to eat when they're only about four weeks old.

Seals move through the water by stroking alternately with their two back flippers.

Plankton, the main food of baleen whales, contains millions of tiny plants and animals.

Among the chief foods in plankton are long, red, shrimplike creatures called krill.

The "whalebone" used to stiffen corsets is actually **baleen** from whales.

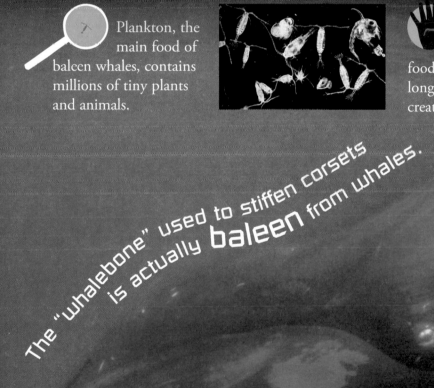

Unlike narwhals and belugas, bowhead whales have no teeth. They filter plankton from vast amounts of water passing through a big fibrous fringe (baleen) in their mouth.

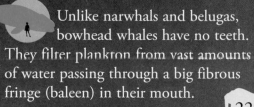

1 Little auks

Midafternoon, and the sky is full of little auks (also called dovekies). They breed in huge numbers in the spring, laying their eggs in sheltered holes and crevices in slopes or cliffs overlooking the sea.

Happy paddling through icy water, a hungry **polar bear** travels from one ice floe to another in search of a plump fish or marine mammal to eat.

Since they've broken into a gallop, these **caribou** have probably been startled, or they sense danger lurking near their herd.

To pounce on his prey hiding in the snow (a vole or a lemming, maybe), this **Arctic fox** springs high up into the air.

Walruses have thick, rough, very wrinkly skin covered with short, coarse hair. They are usually a dark grayish-brown color.

A **snowy owl** cruises the sky looking for lemmings to eat. If there are plenty, these birds live in the Arctic all year. If not, they go south in winter.

Some Arctic birds, like snowy owls, ptarmigans, ravens, and some guillemots, live there all year round; they are called residents. Others, such as geese, ducks, and terns, fly there to breed during the summer months; these birds are known as migrants.

The Arctic tern completes a spectacular migration every year—it flies 22,000 miles (35,400 km) to the Antarctic and back again!

Eider ducks are migrants. They eat mostly shellfish—especially clams, which they crush with their strong bills and swallow whole.

Long-tailed (oldsquaw) ducks, which are very common in the Arctic, have dramatic brown-and-white coloring. They make a lot of noise calling to each other.

Arctic terns live and breed in large groups called colonies.......

When they're not breeding, common guillemots travel over or under the sea to find food. This one is doing his underwater flying trick.

Polar flight

Every so often, every bird in the colony suddenly goes quiet, then—all at once—they all fly away. This phenomenon is known as the "dread."

Snow geese are white, with half-black wings. They breed in the Arctic, but they don't live there all year round.

Beside a glacier, a tern colony breeds and feeds alongside fulmars and kittiwakes, other Arctic birds that get nearly all their food from the sea.

Check out our cool black-and-white feather coats.

Brünnich's guillemots (or thick-billed mürres) breed on rocky cliffs in huge, smelly, noisy, colonies. These birds are strong fliers, but clumsy on takeoff and landing. In fact, they move more easily through water than air.

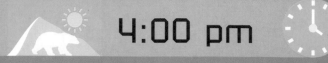

The furry lemming occupies a very important place in the Arctic animal food chain—at the very bottom. Every one of the region's meat-eating mammals and birds see him as a snack. For some, like foxes and snowy owls, he's their main diet, while others turn to lemmings when bigger, meatier prey is not available.

Long-tailed jaegers feed mainly on lemmings; sometimes they steal them from other birds. They even dig in the ground to get into the lemmings' burrow.

I eat mostly plants, but I like to eat the odd insect too.

Because the lemming is a staple food for so many other creatures, animal communities in the Arctic depend on its existence. So, when the lemmings' food is scarce and their numbers fall, the other wildlife suffers as well.

"Please don't see me!"

Collared lemmings grow long winter claws on their front feet so they can dig through the snow for their food.

234

Gyrfalcons need lemmings—when there are lots of lemmings, there are lots of gyrfalcons, too.

Snowy owls eat mostly lemmings, so when there aren't enough of them, snowy numbers drop dramatically.

Ermines may look sweet to us, but lemmings and voles—their chief prey—are terrified of them.

The powerful Arctic wolf preys on everything from caribou and musk oxen to seals, ducks, hares—and especially lemmings.

Small mammals in general—and lemmings in particular—make up the Arctic fox's diet.

Lemmings are a big favorite of the wolverine, but it will eat other small animals—and some very big ones, too!

Mighty musk oxen are the only Arctic creatures who never need to seek shelter, no matter how **bitter** and **blizzardy** it gets. Their name comes from the strong **scent** the males develop during the mating season.

This scary formation is

Coat of many layers

Each musk ox has a covering of coarse, shaggy hair (called guard hair) that hangs down like a long skirt over its stocky body. Underneath this are fine, soft hairs that provide lightweight insulation.

236

This very new calf has bumps where his horns will grow and a coat of short guard hair. Sometimes he keeps warm under his mother's skirt.

Because they're being threatened (probably by wolves or a polar bear), these adults form a circle facing outward, with the youngsters safe inside.

called a "defensive ring."

Communal living

5:02 pm Once snow falls, it forms a crust that lasts until the thaw. In winter, oxen use their hooves to get at the lichen and grass they like to eat.

5:14 pm Adults can run as fast as 25 mph (40 kph). They move fast to escape enemies, and youngsters like to chase each other just for fun.

5:45 pm These males are "jousting"—facing off, backing away, then running at each other and head-butting. They will do this until one gives up.

Beneath their dark, hairy skirts, musk oxen have pale, furry legs.

237

1 Reindeer

Since they've spent the winter in the barren Arctic, these reindeer are very thin, but this may not be due to starvation. Some experts think that when winter approaches, reindeer instinctively eat less to reduce their weight. As a result, they don't need so much food to survive.

Despite being well fed and fat, this **polar bear** has killed a seal. He may eat only its skin and fat, but a hungry bear would strip the bones.

Caribou don't live in the very coldest part of the Arctic, but they wander very far north in spring, when the females (called cows) have their babies.

When a blizzard threatens, this **Arctic fox** protects his face from the cold by wrapping his thick, bushy tail all around his body.

Walruses grunt very loudly when they're fighting or irritated. When a group gathers together, the racket can be heard miles away.

When a **snowy owl** captures prey, she hides it from other hunters by tucking it under her wing. This behavior is called "mantling."

Arctic deer migrate long distances, their hooves are adapted for snow, and males and females both have **antlers**. Members of this species (*Rangifer tarandus*) that live in Europe and Asia are called **reindeer**. Those in North America are **caribou**.

All deer shed their antlers and grow them again every year.

Reindeer and caribou form large herds that travel north in spring, when the young are about to be born, and south in winter, to find food and shelter. Caribou run wild, while reindeer are usually domesticated.

Arctic deer (like this caribou) use their hooves and snouts to get at grasses and lichens under the crusty snow.

Both caribou and reindeer migrate huge distances (up to 600 miles/1,000 km), but reindeer like these are usually accompanied by native human herders.

An Arctic deer's hooves help it to paddle in water and walk on snow. These caribou are crossing a river on the route of their fall migration.

241

Survival of the fiercest

Jaegers are large, aggressive seabirds that eat small mammals, fish, and other birds. This one is tucking into a tasty ptarmigan.

Having hunted and killed a baby hare, this Arctic fox is about to eat him up.

Ferocious wolverines are capable of killing mammals much larger than they are. This one is feeding on a caribou carcass.

To us, the Arctic seems a harsh and cruel place where food is scarce. Many animals survive by hunting, killing, and eating other creatures—a way of life that is common in nature. Animals that do this are known as predators.

Wolves cover huge distances across open icescapes in their search for food.

There's nothing a polar bear likes more than a delicious seal supper on sea ice.

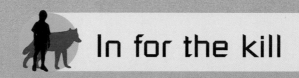

In for the kill

This pack of wolves is chasing a herd of hairy musk oxen at high speed.

The Arctic wolf will hunt and kill more or less any creatures he can find—small ones like ptarmigan, hares, and lemmings, or even musk oxen and caribou, if they're old, sick, or weak from starvation.

When you go outside in the winter, you wear special shoes or boots to keep your feet warm and to stop you from slipping on ice and snow. In the Arctic, animal feet need the same protection as yours would, so nature has provided special adaptations for the harsh environment.

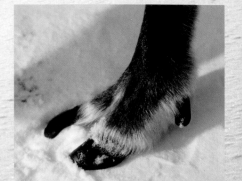

A reindeer's toes spread out, acting like snowshoes to distribute his weight over a wide patch of snow or ice. The feet stay flexible because they're full of soft, fatty tissue.

The Arctic hare's long, silky, white fur covers his whole body, including his legs and feet. In the bitterest cold, hares sit on their back feet, which are insulated with particularly thick, coarse, yellowish fur.

For grip, Arctic hares have clawed toes—four on the back paws and five on the front paws.

When they walk across pack ice, polar bears leave clear tracks. These are very fresh, so the bear can't be far away! . . . .

Humans, polar bears' only predators, use their **tracks** to hunt them.

The ptarmigan's thick feathers reach the tips of his toes to protect him from cold. During the winter, feathers cover even the soles of his feet to enhance his grip.

Even though you can't see them, there are hundreds of tiny, wartlike bumps on the bottom a walrus fin. These help the huge creature to grip onto slippery ice floes.

Polar bears have thick, black, hairless, bumpy pads on the soles and toes of their paws. There are five clawed toes on each paw, with long hair in between.

245

1 Polar bear

At nighttime in April, Arctic light is soft, pinkish, and dim. The Sun is still in the sky, even though it's very low, so animals don't necessarily sleep. Lone polar bears like this one may hunt now, moving slowly and stealthily across large expanses of ice.

When **a polar bear** yawns, you can see that his nose, mouth, and tongue are black. Underneath his white fur, his skin is black too.

In Norway, herds containing thousands of **reindeer** are moving north for the summer— they even travel in heavy snowstorms.

This **Arctic fox's** thick winter coat keeps him cozy. In the summer, his fur is not only a different color—grayish brown— it's much finer, too.

Walrus tusks, which are actually long teeth, help to define a male's status within a group. The ones with big tusks tend to be the leaders.

A **Snowy owl's** big eyes are incredibly powerful— he can see well in the dark, and he can also spot prey on the ground from high in the sky.

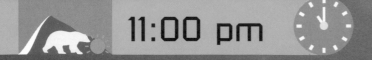
Food can be scarce in the Arctic, so some animals eat what other animals leave behind from a kill. They also feed on the bodies of creatures that have died naturally, or even on human garbage. Occasionally—when starvation threatens—they go even further ...

A hungry wolf sniffs shed antlers in hope of finding a shred of flesh to chew on.

Polar bears strip **whale bones** completely clean— of skin and **blubber** as well as flesh.

Scavenging means eating dead animals or human garbage.

Washed up on an Arctic beach, the carcass of a bowhead whale attracts scavenging polar bears. Although we think of seals as their main food, some experts believe that up to ten percent of their diet is made of whale meat.

Glaucous gulls are very large birds.

Ravens are skilled scavengers that are often found picking at the carcasses of seals and caribou.

It's not only polar bears that eat seals. Glaucous gulls can't kill seals, but they scavenge on dead ones.

On land, Arctic foxes can be found hanging around polar bears. When food is very, very scarce, they sometimes eat bears' droppings.

Wolverines are well suited to scavenging—their powerful jaws and strong neck muscles allow them to crush bones and bite through frozen flesh.

Animals who spend

their lives in the Arctic use up lots of energy just keeping warm, as well as moving around finding food. They need plenty of rest, but because there aren't always light days with dark nights here, they sleep whenever they feel like it.

...This sleepy fox tucks his wet nose under his tail for warmth.

Arctic foxes often wake up late in the evening, since they tend to spend all night hunting for lemmings. When they sleep, they curl themselves into tight balls.

In April, the Arctic can still be colder than your home freezer.

A big slab of sea ice may seem like a funny place to lie down for a nap, but walruses are very comfortable there. They don't have soft fur like polar bears or foxes, but their blubber is so thick and warm that they can sleep soundly on the coldest, hardest bed.

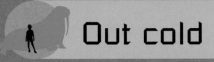

Before he snuggles down for a nap, this polar bear digs out a comfortable hollow in a soft snow bank. Looking on is a pair of foxes hoping to scavenge his leftover food.

Having just made their way through a fierce Arctic snowstorm, a herd of migrating reindeer settles into the fresh snow for a much-needed snooze.

The walruses in the middle of this cozy spoon-fashion group are adults. The ones at the ends, with smaller tusks, are youngsters.

Glossary

Here are some of the important words you will come across as you learn about animals, their habits, and their habitats.

ADOLESCENT a young animal that is no longer a baby, but not yet an adult.

ALGAE simple organisms that grow in water and damp places.

ARBOREAL animals that live most of their lives in trees.

ARID another word for "dry." Arid regions get very little rain.

BALEEN the long fringe made of keratin (the material fingernails are made from) that hangs from the upper jaw of some whales to filter plankton from the water.

BLUBBER the thick layer of fat that some animals (like seals) have to protect them from the cold.

BRACT the modified leaf that grows around a plant's flower.

BREED to produce babies.

BRUSH a layer of shrubs and plants that cover the ground.

BURROW a hole in the ground that an animal lives in. Rabbits and lemmings live in burrows. "Burrow" can also mean the action of digging the hole.

BUTTRESS ROOTS large tree roots that grow above the ground to support a tree and help it absorb extra nutrients when the soil is shallow.

CAMELIDS a group of two-toed mammals that includes camels, dromedaries, llamas, guanacos, vicunas, and alpacas.

CAMOUFLAGE color or markings that allow a living thing to blend in with its surroundings so it's hard to see.

CANOPY the treetop layer of the rain forest. "Canopy" can also refer to the branches and leaves of a single tree.

CARCASS the dead body of an animal, especially one that is used as food.

CARNIVORE an animal that eats meat.

CLAY LICK a clay-rich area like a riverbank. Animals lick clay to help make any poisons they take in with their food less harmful.

CLEANING STATION on a coral reef, a place where fish have their parasites removed by cleaner shrimp or wrasse.

CLOUD FOREST evergreen tropical forest on the lower slopes of a mountain. The forest plants are surrounded by clouds and mist.

COLD BLOODED describes animals that can only control their body temperature by getting near heat or cold (by finding a spot in the sun, for example, or a shady pool).

COLONY a group of animals of the same species that live together.

CORAL material produced by tiny marine polyps that hardens and joins together to form a coral reef. "Coral" also refers to the animal itself.

CREVICE a gap in rock or coral.

DEN a safe resting place dug out of earth (or snow) by a wild, usually predatory, animal. Bears make dens.

DESERT an area that gets very little rainfall. Few plants grow in deserts, which can be warm or cold.

DIURNAL active during the daytime.

DUNG an animal's waste, or droppings.

ECHOLOCATION using echoes to locate objects or prey. Bats, which hunt in the dark, make clicking sounds and listen to the echoes to avoid collisions and find insects.

EGG TOOTH the temporary tooth some baby reptiles and birds use to break out of their eggs. It drops off soon after the baby is out.

EMERGENT a very tall tree that grows above the forest canopy.

FERTILE able to reproduce. Also describes ground or soil that contains lots of plant nutrients.

FLOCK a group of birds that live and fly together.

FOLLICLE a tiny sac-shaped gland containing the root of a hair.

FOOD CHAIN the link between plants and animals in terms of who eats what— for example, plankton turn sunlight into energy, shrimp eat plankton, fish eat shrimp, people eat fish.

FORAGE to search for plants or other food.

FOREST FLOOR the ground layer of the forest.

FREEZING what happens when something gets so cold it turns to ice.

GEYSER A hole in the ground where hot water and steam sometimes shoot out. This happens when volcanic material heats water under the ground.

GILLS the parts of a fish that absorb oxygen from water so it can "breathe."

Glossary

GRAZE to feed on grass or other plants.

GROOMING the way an animal keeps its fur, feathers, or skin clean and free of insects and other pests.

HATCH to break out of its shell, like a baby bird or turtle.

HERBIVORE an animal that eats plants.

HERD a large group of animals that live and travel together. Caribou and gazelles live in herds.

HOOF The foot of a grazing animal such as a horse or buffalo. Hooves are made of keratin, like fingernails.

ICE FLOE a piece of floating sea ice.

INSULATION material used to keep warmth or cold (or sometimes sound) in one place. Blubber and fur provide insulation from cold.

JUVENILE a young animal that is no longer a baby but not yet an adult.

MAMMAL a warm-blooded animal that drinks its mother's milk when it's a baby.

MARINE something connected with the sea.

MARSUPIALS a group of mammals whose females carry their young in a pouch. Kangaroos are marsupials.

MATING the way male and female animals come together to produce young.

MIGRATE to move from one place to another according to the seasons. Animals usually migrate to breed or find food.

MOLT to shed fur, feather, hair, or skin.

NATIVE animals, plants, or people that belong to a particular place. Polar bears are native to the Arctic.

NOCTURNAL active at night.

OASIS a fertile spot in a desert.

OMNIVORE an animal that eats both meat and plants.

PACK a group of animals, such as hyenas and jackals, that live together.

PACK ICE the large masses of ice that result when the frozen sea breaks up.

PARASITE a creature that lives on another creature (called the host), causing it harm or killing it.

PLANKTON the mass of tiny algae and animals that float around in the sea and provide food for fish and marine mammals.

POLLINATION the process of moving pollen between flowers so they can reproduce.

POLYP a simple marine animal such as a coral, sea anemone, or jellyfish. Coral polyps secrete a liquid that becomes hard coral.

POTENT another word for "strong." Snake venom might be described as potent.

PREDATOR an animal that hunts, kills, and eats other animals.

PREY an animal that is hunted, killed, and eaten by other animals.

PROBOSCIS a term based on the Greek for "feed"—now it can just mean "nose." It refers to an elephant's trunk, a monkey's nose, and the tubelike mouthparts some insects use to suck up food.

QUADRUPED having four feet.

RODENTS a family of small mammals like mice that have strong, continually growing, teeth for chewing.

ROOST a place where birds perch to sleep or nest. "Roost" also means the act of settling down to sleep or rest.

SAND DUNE a hill of sand that has been blown into shape by the wind.

SCAVENGER an animal that feeds on the carcasses of other animals, or on human garbage, rather than hunting for itself.

SWARM a dense group of moving animals, usually insects such as locusts or bees.

TALON a bird of prey's sharp claw, which it uses to catch prey.

TENTACLE a long flexible "arm" used by some animals for feeling and grasping. Squid have tentacles.

THERMAL a current of rising warm air. Birds sometimes ride on thermals to gain height or save energy.

TREE LINE the highest level where trees can grow. Above this, it's too cold.

TROPICAL relating to the tropics, the Earth's hot zones near the equator.

UNDERSTORY the forest layer between the floor and the canopy.

VENOM the poisonous liquid injected by some snakes, scorpions, and insects in order to injure or kill prey.

WARM BLOODED describes an animal whose temperature is controlled by its own body.

WHELPING PATCH a sheet of pack ice where a large group of female seals gathers to give birth to their pups.

Index

Acknowledgments

The publisher would like to thank the following for their kind permission to reproduce their photographs:

(Key: a-above; b-below/bottom; c-centre; f-far; l-left; r-right; t-top)

1 FLPA: Jurgen & Christine Sohns. **2 Getty Images:** The Image Bank/Richard Ross (br). **SeaPics.com:** David B. Fleetham (bc). **2-3 Alamy Images:** Steve Bloom Images (b). **Still Pictures:** L. C. Marigo (t). **3 Alamy Images:** Blickwinkel/Hummel (ftr). **Corbis:** Anthony John West (bc). **FLPA:** Tui De Roy/Minden Pictures (tc); Michael & Patricia Fogden/Minden Pictures (tl). **Magnus Elander:** (fbr). **naturepl.com:** Neil Lucas (bl). **4 Alamy Images:** Juniors Bildarchiv/F275 (ca). **Ardea:** Francois Gohier (bl). **FLPA:** Gerard Lacz (br). **5 Scubazoo.com:** Jason Isley (br). **Erwin & Peggy Bauer/Wildstock:** (bl). **6-7 Getty Images:** Robert Harding World Imagery/Sergio Pitamitz. **8 Corbis:** Stephen Fink (bl). **Oceanwide Images:** Gary Bell (tl). **www.wildasia.net:** Terence Lim (crb). **8-9 Oceanwide Images:** Gary Bell. **9 Alamy Images:** Fabrice Bettex (cr). **Corbis:** Stephen Fink (br); Jeffrey L. Rotman (crb). **Scubazoo.com:** Jason Isley (tl). **SeaPics.com:** David B. Fleetham (cra). **Sub Aqua Images/Fredy J. Brauchli:** (tr). **10 SeaPics.com:** Peter Parks/iq-3d (tr, bl). **10-11 SeaPics.com:** Randy Morse (t). **11 SeaPics.com:** Gary Bell (b); Peter Parks/iq-3d (c). **12 Corbis:** Robert Yin (c, tl). **Oceanwide Images:** Gary Bell (l). **12-13 Oceanwide Images:** Gary Bell. **13 Sue Scott:** (b). **SeaPics.com:** Doug Perrine (tr). **www.wildasia.net:** Terence Lim (cl). **14 FLPA:** Chris Newbert/Minden Pictures (cra). **SeaPics.com:** David B. Fleetham; James D. Watt (bl). **Sub Aqua Images/Fredy J. Brauchli:** (cla, br). **15 FLPA:** Chris Newbert/Minden Pictures (cl). **Scubazoo.com:** Jason Isley (br). **SeaPics.com:** James D. Watt (tl). **Sub Aqua Images/Fredy J. Brauchli:** (clb, tr). **16 SeaPics.com:** Doug Perrine (tl). **16-17 SeaPics.com:** Doug Perrine. **17 Jon Bondy:** (crb). **Corbis:** Tom Brakefield (cra). **imagequestmarine.com:** Roger Steene (cr); Scott Tuason (br). **Photolibrary:** Tobias Bernhard (tr). **18 SeaPics.com:** Reinhard Dirscherl (r); Doug Perrine (tl). **www.uwp.no:** Nils Aukan (bl). **18-19 SeaPics.com:** Doug Perrine. **19 Corbis:** Lawson Wood (tl). **SeaPics.com:** Doug Perrine (r). **20 SeaPics.com:** Reinhard Dirscherl (tr). **www.uwp.no:** Nils Aukan (bl). **20-21 Oceanwide Images:** Gary Bell (t, b). **21 Oceanwide Images:** Gary Bell (br, tl). **22 SeaPics.com:** Franco Banfi (tr); Doug Perrine (b). **22-23 SeaPics.com:** Doug Perrine (c). **23 Oceanwide Images:** Gary Bell (tl, cl, cla, tr). **SeaPics.com:** Doug Perrine (b). **24 SeaPics.com:** Doug Perrine (tl). **24-25 SeaPics.com:** Doug Perrine. **25 Corbis:** Bob Abraham (tl); Brandon D. Cole (crb). **imagequestmarine.com:** 2003 James D. Watt (br). **Science Photo Library:** Georgette Douwma (cr). **SeaPics.com:** Doug Perrine (cra). **Sub Aqua Images/Fredy J. Brauchli:** (tr). **26 Corbis:** (cla) Stephen Fink (bl); Stuart Westmorland (cr). **27 Corbis:** (b) Stuart Westmorland (cra). **SeaPics.com:** David B. Fleetham (tl); Doug Perrine (cl). **28 Corbis:** Darrell Gulin (cl). **NHPA/Photoshot:** B. Jones & M. Shimlock (bl). **28-29 FLPA:** Norbert Wu/Minden Pictures. **29 Alamy Images:** S.C. Bisserot/Worldwide Picture Library (crb). **Corbis:** Martin Harvey (br). **FLPA:** Shin Yoshino/Minden Pictures (cl). **Science Photo Library:** Georgette Douwma (cra). **SeaPics.com:** Doug Perrine (tr). **30 Sub Aqua Images/Fredy J. Brauchli:** (tl). **30-31 Corbis:** Lawson Wood (cb). **Sub Aqua Images/Fredy J. Brauchli:** (b). **31 Corbis:** Lawson Wood (br). **www.wildasia.net:** Terence Lim (tr, cl). **32 Oceanwide Images:** Gary Bell (bl, clb). **Norbert Wu:** (tr). **32-33 Norbert Wu. 33 Jon Bondy:** (crb). **imagequestmarine.com:** Roger Steene (cr). **Photolibrary:** (tr). **Scubazoo.com:** Jason Isley (cra, br, cl). **34 Sue Scott:** (br). **SeaPics.com:** Doug Perrine (bl). **35 Corbis:** Lawson Wood (tr). **Sue Scott:** (cl, br, clb). **www.wildasia.net:** Terence Lim (ca). **36 Photolibrary:** Dave Fleetham (br). **Scubazoo.com:** Jason Isley. **SeaPics.com:** Mark Strickland (bl). **Treasure Images:** Eric Madeja (cla). **37 Photolibrary:** Dave Fleetham (cl). **SeaPics.com:** Mark Strickland (br); James D. Watt (cra). **Treasure Images:** Eric Madeja (tl). **38 SeaPics.com:** Reinhard Dirscherl (b, tl). **39 Corbis:** Amos Nachoum (br). **Dr Frances Dipper:** (clb) (bl). **National Geographic Stock:** David Doubilet (t). **SeaPics.com:** Shedd Aquar/Ceisel (cr). **40 Corbis:** Lawson Wood (bl). **FLPA:** Norbert Wu/Minden Pictures (cla). **Science Photo Library:** Matthew Oldfield, Scubazoo (tl). **40-41 Science Photo Library:** Matthew Oldfield, Scubazoo. **41 Alamy Images:** Fabrice Bettex (cr). **Ardea:** Valerie Taylor (tr). **Jon Bondy:** (crb). **FLPA:** Norbert Wu/Minden Pictures (bl). **Scubazoo.com:** Jason Isley (br). **SeaPics.com:** Doug Perrine (cra). **42 Corbis:** Stephen Frink (b). **42-43 Alamy Images:** James D Watt/Stephen Fink Collection. **43 Getty Images:** Gary Bell (br); David Hall (tr). **44 Corbis:** Lawson Wood. **FLPA:** Norbert Wu/Minden Pictures (tr). **Norbert Wu:** (b). **45 Corbis:** Jeffrey L. Rotman (bl); Douglas P. Wilson/Frank Lane Picture Agency (tl). **FLPA:** Norbert Wu/Minden Pictures (tr). **naturepl.com:** Georgette Douwma (br). **46 Science Photo Library:** Alexis Rosenfeld (clb, bl). **SeaPics.com:** Doug Perrine (tl). **46-47 SeaPics.com:** Doug Perrine. **47 Corbis:** Kevin Schafer (tl). **48-49 NHPA/Photoshot:** Martin Wendler. **50 Alamy Images:** (tl). **50-51 Alamy Images. 51 Alamy Images:** (crb). **Ardea:** (cra). **FLPA:** (br). **OSF:** (tr). **stevebloom.com:** (cr). **52 Ardea:** (tl). **Corbis:** Theo Allofs (bl). **53 Corbis:** Kevin Schafer/Zefa. **Still Pictures:** (tr). **54 Alamy Images:** (r). **Ardea:** (bl). **naturepl.com:** (tl). **55 Alamy Images:** (tl). **FLPA:** (r). **NHPA/Photoshot:** (bl). **56 Fauna & Flora International:** (r). **FLPA:** (tl, clb). **NHPA/Photoshot:** (cl). **57 Fauna & Flora International:** (tl). **FLPA:** (tr, cra). **OSF:** (br). **Photolibrary:** Oxford Scientific (crb). **58 Getty Images:** Image Bank (tl). **OSF:** (bl, tl). **Science Photo Library:** (tr). **59 Alamy Images:** (crb). **Corbis:** (cr). **FLPA:** (cra). **NHPA/Photoshot:** (tl). **Still Pictures:** (br). **60 naturepl.com. 61 Corbis:** Michael & Patricia Fogden (br). **FLPA:** (tr, cra, crb). **62 FLPA:** (l, tr). **Lonely Planet Images:** (br). **63 Alamy Images:** (tl); Brand X Pictures (br). **NHPA/Photoshot:** (bl). **Still Pictures:** (tr). **64 FLPA:** (l, r). **65 Ardea:** (br). **FLPA:** (l, tr). **66 NHPA/Photoshot:** (tl). **67 FLPA:** (tr, br, cr). **OSF:** (crb). **Still Pictures:** (cra). **68 Corbis:** Michael & Patricia Fogden (br). **FLPA:** (cra). **Photolibrary:** (bl). **68-69 Photolibrary:** (background). **69 Alamy Images:** (tl). **Corbis:** Michael & Patricia Fogden (tr). **FLPA:** (cra, b, crb). **70 Arco Images:** (r). **Corbis:** (tl); Arthur Morris (br). **NHPA/Photoshot:** (bl). **71 Corbis:** Michael & Patricia Fogden (tr). **72 FLPA:** (tl). **Photolibrary:** (br). **73 Corbis:** Michael & Patricia Fogden (b). **FLPA:** (tl). **Photolibrary:** (tr). **74 Corbis:** Galen Rowell (tl). **75 Alamy Images:** (cr). **Corbis:** Tim Davis (tr). **Das Fotoarchiv:** (crb). **naturepl.com:** (br). **NHPA/Photoshot:** (cra). **76 Alamy Images:** (tl). **NHPA/Photoshot:** (cla, bl, clb). **Photolibrary:** (r). **77 Corbis:** Gary Braasch (b/background). **FLPA:** (tr). **Photolibrary:** (l). **78 Alamy Images:** (cl). **FLPA:** (cla). **naturepl.com:** (clb, bl, r). **Photolibrary:** (tl). **79 naturepl.com:** (br). **OSF:** (tr, cra). **80 naturepl.com:** (r). **OSF:** (bl). **81 Ardea:** (cra). **FLPA:** (br). **Photolibrary:** (cr). **82 FLPA:** (b, tl). **naturepl.com:** (cb, tfl). **83 FLPA:** (tr, br, cr). **NHPA/Photoshot:** (cra). **Photolibrary:** (crb). **84 FLPA:** (l, br). **85 FLPA:** (tl). **Getty Images:** (br). **National Geographic Stock:** (tr). **Science Photo Library:** (fbl, bl). **86 OSF:** (t, bl). **87 NHPA/Photoshot:** (tr). **OSF:** (c). **Photolibrary:** (tl, br). **89 FLPA:** (bl). **Photolibrary:** (r). **89 OSF:** (tr). **Photolibrary:** (br). **90-91 FLPA:** David Hosking. **92 Alamy Images:** Steve Bloom Images (tl). **92-93 Alamy Images:** Steve Bloom Images. **93 Ardea:** Peter Steyn (crb). **Corbis:** Marcello Calandrini (cr); Martin Harvey (br); Martin Harvey; Gallo Images (tr). **FLPA:** Michael & Patricia Fogden/Minden Pictures (cra). **94 Alamy Images:** Steve Bloom Images (l, cb). **94-95 Alamy Images:** Steve Bloom Images (c). **95 Corbis:** Tim Davis (cra); Mary Ann McDonald (cr); Paul A. Souders (tr). **Getty Images:** Daryl Balfour (cb). **96-97 Alamy Images:** Steve Bloom Images. **97 Ardea:** Joanna Van Gruisen (br). **Bruce Coleman Ltd:** Carol Hughes (crb). **Corbis:** Tom Brakefield (tr). **naturepl.com:** Herman Brehm (cra). **98 Alamy Images:** Steve Bloom Images (tl). **Corbis:** Mary Ann McDonald (bl). **98-99 naturepl.com:** Richard du Toit. **99 Ardea:** Chris Harvey (crb). **Corbis:** Lynda Richardson (cra); Ron Sanford (cr). **Getty Images:** Jonathan & Angela (tr). **100 Wynand & Claudia Du Plessis:** (tl). **100-101 Wynand & Claudia Du Plessis. 101 Alamy Images:** Steve Bloom Images (br). **Corbis:** Roger Tidman (crb). **Getty Images:** Peter Lilja (tr). **naturepl.com:** Terry Andrewartha (cr). **102 DK Images:** Jerry Young (tl). **Still Pictures:** Heike Fischer (bl). **102-103 Photolibrary:** Osolinski Stan (c). **103 Corbis:** Gallo Images (tr); Clem Haagner; Gallo Images (crb). **Still Pictures:** Martin Harvey (cra). **104 Corbis:** Gallo Images (l); Wolfgang Kaehler (br). **105 Corbis:** Rick Doyle (cr); Wolfgang Kaehler (br, bl). **106 Corbis:** Nigel J. Dennis; Gallo Images (tl, br); Wolfgang Kaehler (bl). **107 Corbis:** Steve Bein (tl); Gavin G. Thomson/Gallo Images (tr); Winifred Wisniewski; Frank Lane Picture Agency (b). **108 Photolibrary:** Michael Fogden (tl). **108-109 Photolibrary:** Michael Fogden. **109 Corbis:** Yann Arthus-Bertrand (tr); Matin Harvey (cr); William Manning (cra). **FLPA:** William S. Clark (crb). **Getty Images:** Gallo Images/Heinrich van den Berg (br). **110 Corbis:** Peter Johnson (cl). **Getty Images:** Gallo Images/Daryl Balfour (b). **110-111 Corbis:** Roger De La Harpe/Gallo Images (c). **111 Corbis:** Peter Johnson (tr). **Getty Images:** Darrell Gulin (b). **112 Alamy Images:** David Wall (tl). **Corbis:** Joe McDonald (bl). **113 Corbis:** Nigel J. Dennis/Gallo Images (tl, tr). **DK Images:** Jerry Young (crb). **naturepl.com:** Richard du Toit (br). **114 Ardea:** Clem Haagner (br). **Corbis:** Richard du Toit/Gallo Images (tl). **National Geographic Stock:** Volkmar K. Wentzel (bl). **115 Alamy Images:** Steve Bloom Images (tl). **Ardea:** Clem Haagner (bl). **Corbis:** Peter Johnson (br). **naturepl.com:** Sharon Heald (cra); Richard du Toit (crb). **116 National Geographic Stock:** Chris Johns (l). **116-117 National Geographic Stock:** Mattias Klum (bc). **117 National Geographic Stock:** Mattias Klum (br). **Roberta Stacey:** (tl). **118 Alamy Images:** Steve Bloom Images (tl). **Getty Images:** Gallo Images/Heinrich van den Berg (bl). **118-119 Alamy Images:** Steve Bloom Images. **119 Alamy Images:** Steve Bloom Images (br). **Corbis:** Darrell Gulin (cr). **Getty Images:** James Balog (tr). **National Geographic Stock:** Chris Johns (cra). **Photolibrary:** Alan Hartley (crb). **120 DK Images:** Philip Dowell (clb). **120-121 National Geographic Stock:** Chris Johns (b). **121 Bruce Coleman Ltd:** Christer Fredriksson (r). **naturepl.com:** Richard du Toit (cl). **122 Corbis:** Martin Harvey/Gallo Images (bl). **122-123 Corbis:** Martin Harvey/Gallo Images (cb). **123 Alamy Images:** Martin Harvey (tr, tl). **Corbis:** Gallo Images (cla, cl, clb). **Getty Images:** Jonathan & Angela Scott (br). **124 NHPA/Photoshot:** Jonathan & Angela Scott (l). **124-125 Corbis:** Jeffrey L. Rotman (b). **125 Ardea:** Clem Haagner (br). **National Geographic Stock:** Kim Wolhuter (tl). **naturepl.com:** Sharon Heald (cr); Ron O'Connor (crb). **126 Alamy Images:** Steve Bloom Images (tl). **127 Alamy Images:** Steve Bloom Images (br, cl, cr). **Corbis:** Roger Tidman (crb). **Getty Images:** Stuart Westmorland (cra). **naturepl.com:** Peter Blackwell (tr). **128 Corbis:** Peter Johnson (br); David A. Northcott (tr). **National Geographic Stock:** Kim Wolhuter (bl). **128-129 Corbis:** David A. Northcott (t). **129 Corbis:** Hein von Horsten/Gallo Images (r); Peter Johnson (bl); George McCarthy (b). **130 Getty Images:** Blake Little (b). **131 Alamy Images:** Steve Bloom (tl). **Bruce Coleman Ltd:** John Shaw (b). **132-133 FLPA:** Bob Gibbons. **134-135 Alain & Berny Sebe/www.alainsebeimages.com. 135 Ardea:** Duncan Usher (cb). **FLPA:** Yossi Eshbol (t); Chris Mattison (ca). **Getty Images:** National Geographic/Michael Melford (c); National Geographic/Carsten Peter (br). **136 FLPA:** Mark Moffett/Minden (tr); Konrad Wothe/Minden (b). **Alain & Berny Sebe/www.alainsebeimages.com:** (c). **137 Ardea:** Ken Lucas (tl). **FLPA:** David Hosking (bl). **NHPA/Photoshot:** Martin Harvey (br). **138 Alamy Images:** David Hosking. **139 Alamy Images:** Krys Bailey (crb). **Still Pictures:** Roland Seitre (t). **140 Getty Images:** Digital Vision/Digital Zoo (t). **naturepl.com:** Bernard Castelein (bl). **NHPA/Photoshot:** Daniel Heuclin (br). **141 Eyal Bartov:** (bl). **FLPA:** David Hosking (tl). **Lonely Planet Images:** Olivier Cirendini (r). **NHPA/Photoshot:** Daniel Heuclin (br). **142-143 Alain & Berny Sebe/www.alainsebeimages.com. 143 Alamy Images:** Blickwinkel (ca). **Corbis:** Craig Aurness (br). **OSF:** Waina Cheng (crb). **Science Photo Library:** George D. Lepp (cr). **Still Pictures:** Alain Dragesco-Joffe (tr). **144 Getty Images:** Frans Lemmens (tl). **NHPA/Photoshot:** Daniel Heuclin (bl). **144-145 Natural Visions:** Jason Venus. **145 Alamy Images:** Gary Cook (br). **NHPA/Photoshot:** Daniel Heuclin (tr, cra); Karl Switak (crb). **146 FLPA:** Mitsuaki Iwago/Minden (bl). **naturepl.com:** Anup Shah (tr). **146-147 naturepl.com:** Vincent Munier. **147 FLPA:** Mitsuaki Iwago/Minden (ca); Sunset (cb). **naturepl.com:** Karl Ammann (br). **148 Raymonde Bonnefille/sahara-nature.com:** (bl). **FLPA:** Gerry Ellis/Minden (br). **148-149 NHPA/Photoshot:** Daniel Heuclin. **149 Raymonde Bonnefille/sahara-nature.com:** (tl). **150-151 Alamy Images:** Iconotec. **151 Alamy Images:** Blickwinkel (cra). **Corbis:** (cr). **Still Pictures:** Alain Dragesco-Joffe (tr, crb); Frans Lemmens (br). **152-153 Corbis:** Frans Lemmens. **153 fjexpeditions.com/Andras Zboray:** (tr). **154 FLPA:** Hans Schouten (tr). **naturepl.com:** Hanne & Jens Eriksen. **NHPA/Photoshot:** (c). **154-155 FLPA:** Konrad Wothe/Foto Natura. **155 FLPA:** Duncan Usher (tl). **OSF:** Manfred Pfefferle (tr). **Alain & Berny Sebe/www.alainsebeimages.com:** (cr). **Still Pictures:** Alain Dragesco-Joffe (cl). **157 Alamy Images:** David J Slater (crb). **Ardea:** Ian Beames (tr). **naturepl.com:** Hanne & Jens Eriksen (br); Neil Lucas (cra); Anup Shah (cr). **158 FLPA:** Gerry Ellis/Minden (tr). **158-159 Imagestate:** Philippe Saharoff/Explorer. **159 Alain & Berny Sebe/www.alainsebeimages.com:** (cl). **Still Pictures:** Patricia Jordan (br). **160 Still Pictures:** Martin Harvey (l). **160-161 Science Photo Library:** Alan and Sandy Carey. **161 OSF:** Alain Dragesco-Joffe (cr, br). **Still Pictures:** Alain Dragesco-Joffe (tr). **162 www.geres-asso.org/Michel Aymerich:** (tl). **162-163 fjexpeditions.com/Andras Zboray. 163 fjexpeditions.com/Andras Zboray:** (tr, br, cr). **FLPA:** Chris Mattison (tl). **165 Getty Images:** National Geographic/Carsten Peter (br). **NHPA/Photoshot:** Daniel Heuclin (cra); Christophe Ratier (crb). **Robert Harding Picture Library:** (cr). **166 FLPA:** Yossi Eshbol (bl). **166-167 OSF:** Alain Dragesco-Joffe. **167 Alamy Images:** David Hosking (tr). **alsirhan.com. OSF:** Alain Dragesco-Joffe (tl). **Still Pictures:** Alain Dragesco-Joffe (br). **168 FLPA:** David Hosking (bl). **OSF:** Eyal Bartov (cl). **168-169 NHPA/Photoshot:** Daniel Heuclin. **169 Alamy Images:** Malie Rich-Griffith (tr). **Still Pictures:** Frans Lemmens (br). **Erwin & Peggy Bauer/Wildstock:** (tl). **170 NHPA/Photoshot:** Daniel Heuclin (c). **OSF:** IFA-Bilderteam Gmbh (b). **170-171 Alain & Berny Sebe/www.alainsebeimages.com. 171 www.geres-asso.org/Michel Aymerich:** (cr, bl). **NHPA/Photoshot:** Daniel Heuclin (tl). **172-173 Alamy Images:** Craig Lovell/Eagle Visions Photography. **174 Alamy Images:** Jan Baks (tl). **174-175 Alamy Images:** Jan Baks. **175 FLPA:** Tui De Roy/Minden Pictures (t); Tim Fitzharris/Minden Pictures (b). **naturepl.com:** Jim Clare (ca); Gabriel Rojo (cb). **Photolibrary:** Mark Jones/Oxford Scientific (c). **176 Alamy Images:** Les Gibbon (br). **Ardea:** François Gohier (l). **FLPA:** Tui De Roy/Minden Pictures (cr, cra). **176-177 Photolibrary:** Oxford Scientific. **177 naturepl.com:** Hans Christoph Kappel (tr); Pete Oxford (cr). **NHPA/Photoshot:** Otto Pfister (tl, b). **178 Alamy Images:** Kevin Schafer (r). **naturepl.com:** John Waters (tl). **NHPA/Photoshot:** Image Quest 3-D (cl). **179 Alamy Images:** Kevin Schafer (tl). **naturepl.com:** Gabriel Rojo (tr). **180 FLPA:** Tui de Roy (tl). **180-181 FLPA:** Tui de Roy. **181 Ardea:** François Gohier (t). **FLPA:** Tui De Roy/Minden Pictures (ca, cb). **NHPA/Photoshot:** Laurie Campbell (b); Kevin Schafer (c). **182 FLPA:** Yva Momatiuk/John Eastcott/Minden Pictures (br); Jurgen & Christine Sohns (bl). **naturepl.com:** David Tipling (c). **182-183 naturepl.com:** Daniel Gomez. **183 FLPA:** John Hawkins (cl); Hans Hut/Foto Natura (bl); Frans Lanting/Minden Pictures (clb); R & M Van Nostrand (t); Tom Vezo/Minden Pictures (cr); Tony Wharton (br). **naturepl.com:** Gabriel Rojo (tc). **184 FLPA:** Tui de Roy (bl). **184-185 Ardea:** François Gohier. **185 Natural Science Photos:** A. Mercieca (t). **186 Corbis:** Wolfgang Kaehler (tl). **NHPA/Photoshot:** Laurie Campbell (bl). **186-187 FLPA:** Winfried Wisniewski. **187 FLPA:** Tui De Roy/Minden Pictures (tl); Pete Oxford/Minden Pictures (tc). **NHPA/Photoshot:** Laurie Campbell (bc); Jany Sauvanet (tr). **188 Corbis:** Anthony John West (t). **188-189 Corbis:** Anthony John West. **189 Alamy Images:** Edward Parker (ca). **Laurie Campbell Photography:** (c). **FLPA:** (b); Tui De Roy/Minden Pictures (t). **naturepl.com:** Mike Potts (cb). **190 Andres Morya Photography:** (bl). **Corbis:** (tl). **naturepl.com:** Pete Oxford (cra). **190-191 Getty Images:** Posing Productions (b). **191 Getty Images:** Robert Harding World Imagery (tl). **naturepl.com:** Luiz Claudio Marigo (r). **Professor Wayne A. Wurtsbaugh, Aquatic, Watershed and Earth Resources Dept./Ecology Center:** (c). **192 FLPA:** Tui De Roy/Minden Pictures (bl). **naturepl.com:** Hanne Jens Eriksen (cla). **192-193 naturepl.com:** Rhonda Klevansky (t); Gabriel Rojo (b). **193 FLPA:** Tui De Roy/Minden Pictures (cr). **naturepl.com:** Colin Seddon. **NHPA/Photoshot:** Lady Phillipa Scott (tr); Dave Watts (tc). **194 Corbis:** Bob Rowan/Progressive Image (bl); Hubert Stadler (tr). **194-195 naturepl.com:** Doug Allan. **195 Alamy Images:** Homer Sykes (tr). **Corbis:** Hubert Stadler (tl). **naturalimagebank.com/Mark Levesley:** (br). **naturepl.com:** Doug Allan (b). **196 Laurie Campbell Photography:** (t). **196-197 Laurie Campbell Photography. 197 Corbis:** Kevin Schafer (ca). **FLPA:** Tui De Roy/Minden Pictures (t, cb); Pete Oxford/Minden Pictures (c). **NHPA/Photoshot:** T Kitchin & V Hurst (b). **198 Evan Bowen-Jones/Fauna & Flora International:** (r). **National Geographic Stock:** Joel Sartore (bl). **199 Alamy Images:** Michele Falzone (cr); J Marshall - Tribaleye Images (crb). **FLPA:** Tui De Roy/Minden Pictures (b). **National Geographic Stock:** Joel Sartore (tl). **Still Pictures:** Juan Carlos Munoz (tr). **200 Getty Images:** Purestock (bl). **Natural Science Photos:** R Kemp (c). **201 Alamy Images:** Terry Whittaker (tc). **Corbis:** Kevin Schafer (tl). **NHPA/Photoshot:** Jany Sauvanet (tr). **202 FLPA:** Jurgen & Christine Sohns (l). **202-203 Corbis:** W. Perry Conway (b). **203 Laurie Campbell Photography:** (cr). **Getty Images:** National Geographic (crb). **NHPA/Photoshot:** T Kitchin & V Hurst (tr); John Shaw (b). **204 FLPA:** Tui De Roy/Minden Pictures (br, tl). **Paul Souders/WorldFoto:** (t). **204-205 Paul Souders/WorldFoto. 205 Alamy Images:** Simon Littlejohn (b). **Laurie Campbell Photography:** (c). **naturepl.com:** Daniel Gomez (cb); Pete Oxford (t). **Robert Harding Picture Library:** Pete Oxford (ca). **206 Alamy Images:** Arco Images (l). **FLPA:** Pete Oxford (cr). **207 Corbis:** (t). **FLPA:** Mark Newman (crb). **naturepl.com:** Jim Clare (tr). **NHPA/Photoshot:** Kevin Schafer (b); Dave Watts (l). **208 Alamy Images:** Javier Etcheverry (tr). **FLPA:** Hugh Clark (br). **NHPA/Photoshot:** Karl Switak (bl). **209 FLPA:** Gerry Ellis/Minden Pictures (r). **210 Ardea:** Chris Harvey (t). **FLPA:** Tui De Roy/Minden Pictures (c). **NHPA/Photoshot:** T Kitchin & V Hurst (b). **211 Alamy Images:** Holger Ehlers (tr). **FLPA:** Foto Natura Stock (cl). **naturepl.com:** Gabriel Rojo (br, cb); Colin Seddon (tl). **212-213 National Geographic Stock:** Ralph Lee Hopkins. **214 Corbis:** Frank Lukasseck/Zefa. **214-215 Corbis:** Frank Lukasseck/Zefa. **215 Alamy Images:** Bryan And Cherry Alexander Photography (tr); Mark Duffy (br). **naturepl.com:** Terry Andrewartha (cr); Steve Kazlowski (cra); Tom Mangelsen (crb). **216 Corbis:** Tom Brakefield/Zefa (bl). **216-217 Corbis:** Dan Guravich. **217 Corbis:** Dan Guravich (tr). **218 Ardea:** Sid Roberts (tl). **Corbis:** Alan & Sandy Carey/Zefa (bl). **FLPA:** Winifried Wisniewski/Foto Natura (tr). **218-219 Magnus Elander. 219 Ardea:** M. Watson (tl). **OSF:** Norbert Rosing (tr). **220 AlaskaStock.com:** (c) 2006 Steven Kazlowski (bl). **FLPA:** Jim Brandenburgh/Minden Pictures. **221 Alamy Images:** Image State (cr); Juniors Bildarchiv (tr). **FLPA:** Michio Hoshino/Minden Pictures (br). **222 Alamy Images:** John Schwieder (bl). **222-223 Alamy Images:** Steve Bloom Images. **223 Magnus Elander:** (t, c, cl, cr). **224 Magnus Elander:** (tl). **224-225 Magnus Elander. 225 Alamy Images:** Bryan And Cherry Alexander Photography (tl); Steven J. Kazlowski (tr). **Ardea:** Doc White (crb). **Corbis:** Theo Allofs (cr). **naturepl.com:** Niall Benvie (br); Asgeir Helgestad (cra). **226 Still Pictures:** Kevin Schafer (tr). **226-227 Alamy Images:** Bryan And Cherry Alexander Photography (c); Steven J. Kazlowski. **227 Alamy Images:** blickwinkel (tr); Steven J. Kazlowski (br). **Magnus Elander:** (tl). **228 Alamy Images:** David Fleetham (tl). **Corbis:** Philip James Corwin (cr); Sea World of California (b). **229 Corbis:** Douglas Wilson/FLPA (cl). **FLPA:** Flip Nicklin/Minden Pictures (b). **OSF:** Doug Allen (t). **230 Alamy Images:** Bryan And Cherry Alexander Photography. **230-231 Alamy Images:** Bryan And Cherry Alexander Photography. **231 Alamy Images:** Steven J. Kazlowski (cr). **FLPA:** Ron Austing (br); Jim Brandenburgh/Minden Pictures (cra). **Getty Images:** Pal Hermansen (tr). **Still Pictures:** Kelvin Aitken (crb). **232 Alamy Images:** D.Kjaer/The National Trust Photo Library (tl). **Bryan and Cherry Alexander Photography:** (bl). **FLPA:** Flip de Nooyer/Foto Natura (cl); John Watkins (clb). **232-233 FLPA:** David Hosking. **233 Corbis:** Stuart Westmorland (br). **FLPA:** Winifried Wisniewski (tr). **234 Alamy Images:** blickwinkel (tr). **Ardea:** Andrey Zvoznikor (bl). **234-235 naturepl.com:** Mike Potts. **235 Alamy Images:** Arco Images (br); Visual & Written SL (tl, cr). **Corbis:** Staffon Widstrand (bl). **FLPA:** Konrad Wothe/Minden Pictures (tr). **naturepl.com:** Tom Mangelsen (cra). **236 Alamy Images:** Steven J. Kazlowski (bl). **236-237 Bryan and Cherry Alexander Photography:** (b). **237 Alamy Images:** Juniors Bildarchiv (tr, br); Steven J. Kazlowski (tl). **Bryan and Cherry Alexander Photography:** (cr). **238 Corbis:** Hans Reinhard/Zefa (tl). **238-239 Corbis:** Hans Reinhard/Zefa. **239 Alamy Images:** blickwinkel (crb). **Ardea:** John Swedberg (cra). **naturepl.com:** Andrey Zvoznikov (br). **SuperStock:** age foto stock (tr). **240 OSF:** Mark Hamblin (bl). **241 Alamy Images:** Bryan And Cherry Alexander Photography (br); Marco Regalia (tr). **FLPA:** Yva Momatiuk/John Eastcott/Minden Pictures (tl). **242 Alamy Images:** Steven J. Kazlowski (tl, clb). **Corbis:** Tom Brakefield (cla). **242-243 FLPA:** Jim Brandenburgh/Minden Pictures. **243 Corbis:** Jacques Langevin/Sygma (t/background). **FLPA:** Jim Brandenburgh/Minden Pictures (t, b); Yva Momatiuk/John Eastcott/Minden Pictures (tl). **244 Alamy Images:** Arco Images (tc). **Magnus Elander:** (bl). **244-245 Bryan and Cherry Alexander Photography. 245 FLPA:** Flip Nicklin/Minden PIctures (br). **Magnus Elander:** (tr). **246 Alamy Images:** Steve Bloom Images. **246-247 Alamy Images:** Steve Bloom Images. **247 Alamy Images:** Steven J. Kazlowski (tr, crb). **Corbis:** George D. Lepp (cr). **naturepl.com:** Asgeir Helgestad (cra). **Science Photo Library:** E. R. Degginger (br). **248 Alamy Images:** Arco Images (tr). **248-249 Alamy Images:** Steven J. Kazlowski. **249 Alamy Images:** Bryan And Cherry Alexander Photography (tr, cr). **Corbis:** Uwe Walz (tl). **OSF:** Daniel Cox (br). **250 naturepl.com:** Mark Payne-Gill (tr). **250-251 FLPA:** Rinie Van Muers/Foto Natura. **251 Bryan and Cherry Alexander Photography:** (tl). **naturepl.com:** Asgeir Helgestad (tr). **252-253 Corbis:** Frank Lukasseck. **254-255 naturepl.com:** Daniel Gomez. **256 FLPA:** Frans Lanting/Minden Pictures.

All other images © Dorling Kindersley
For further information see: www.dkimages.com

Dorling Kindersley would like to thank:
Rob Nunn for picture research, and Wendy Horobin and Penny Smith for proofreading.